DEDICATION

America's Patriot Pastors

You were mighty men of courage planting the Biblical seeds of liberty throughout the colonies, and also men of action who secured religious liberty for generations to come. May we learn from and emulate your example.

America's Founding Fathers

You launched the most successful nation in history. May our generation honor your wisdom and sacrifice by preserving the Torch of Freedom for future generations.

PREFACE

This Workbook is your easy to use note-taking tool during the classroom presentation of ***BIBLICAL CITIZENSHIP IN MODERN AMERICA.***

As a registered member of the class, you also have access to a digital version of the workbook when you login at BiblicalCitizens.com.

This 8-Week course includes commentary from many notable pastors, constitutional experts, historians, and others; as well as an abbreviated version of ***CONSTITUTION ALIVE!***, which is a more extensive course on the Constitution.

Each week, we'll begin with an introduction to the week's class and then take a journey through the Bible & American history to rediscover the secret sauce that produces a prosperous society when Biblical principles are applied. We will visit experts across the Nation, visit the amazing library of David Barton where we'll find the world's largest private collection of America's Founding Era documents, and then we'll dive into the U.S. Constitution in the very room where it was framed – Independence Hall in Philadelphia, Pennsylvania.

If you would like to host this class at your church, in your home, online, or any other location, please visit BiblicalCitizens.com for more information.

WORKBOOK CONTENTS

Week 1:   The Foundation 7

Week 2:   Tending the Garden 11

Week 3:   Understanding the Times 17

Week 4:   The Seeds of Liberty.. 25

Week 5:   Who Has Authority to Decide?................... 41

Week 6:   Of Kings & Courts 49

Week 7:   Religious Liberty & Other Rights............... 61

Week 8:   Being Salt & Light... 69

Appendix A: U.S. Constitution at a Glance 75

Appendix B: What About Separation of Church & State? ..79

Appendix C: The Declaration of Independence 87

Appendix D: Endnotes.. 93
                Answer Key 98

Appendix E: The Constitution Made Easy 109

WEEK ONE
The Foundation

Therefore go and make disciples of all nations, baptizing them in the name of the Father and of the Son and of the Holy Spirit, and teaching them to obey everything I have commanded you. And surely I am with you always, to the very end of the age.

- Matthew 28:19-20

The Great Commission is to make _____ [1] of all _____ [2] and to teach them to obey _____ [3] Jesus commanded.

The instruction manual for life is _____ _____. [4]

All the miseries and evils which men suffer from vice, crime, ambition, injustice, oppression, slavery and war, proceed from their despising or neglecting the precepts contained in the Bible.

- Noah Webster

Who is Caesar in America? ____ ____ _____ [5]

The church must take right ground in regard to politics. Politics are part of a religion in a country as this, and Christians must do their duty to their country as a part of their duty to God. God will bless or curse this nation according to the course Christians take in politics.   **- Charles Finney**

If anyone, then, knows the good they ought to do and doesn't do it, it is sin for them.   **- James 4:17**

No free government, nor the blessings of liberty, can be preserved to any people but by a _____ _____[6] *to fundamental principles.*   **- George Mason**

According to President James Garfield, who is to blame when we have a Congress that is out of control and foolish? _____[7]

Now, more than ever before, the people are responsible for the character of their Congress. If that body be ignorant, reckless, and corrupt, it is because the people tolerate ignorance, recklessness, and corruption. If it be intelligent, brave, and pure, it is because the people demand these high qualities to represent them in the national legislature.... If the next centennial does not find us a great nation ... it will be because those who represent the enterprise, the culture, and the morality of the nation do not aid in controlling the political forces.[i]

- President James Garfield

A free and just society must begin with a faith in the _____ _____ _____.[8]

The four aspects of Faith are manifested through what key facets?

1. _____   3. _____

2. _____   4. _____[9]

Morality is a standard not to be imposed externally by a king, tyrant or government; instead, it is to begin internally by a transformation of the _____[10].

Once you have good morality, and you know what is good and what is evil, then you can make _____ _____[11] in your nation.

Man's laws must line up under _____ _____[12] or they are not good laws.

Laws in a society should be balanced on _____ and _____.[13]

Liberty man is equipped by wearing the _____ _____[14] of God.

Once you've educated your children in a Biblical worldview and morality, the result is _____.[15]

Liberty man looks over the Atlantic Ocean ready to defend his _____, _____, good _____,[16] and the ability to train up his children in the way they should go.

The family of Faith is the church, it's _____ and _____.[17] God has called us to rebuild the ideals of this monument into every aspect of culture and to _____[18] these ideals to their maximum beauty and glory.

_____

_____

_____

_____

_____

_____

_____

_____

_____

_____

_____

_____

_____

_____

_____

WEEK TWO
Tending The Garden

Genesis is often known as the _____ _____[1] of the Bible because every single major teaching goes back to the book of Genesis.

The first form of government is _____ _____[2].

The three institutions of government in Scripture are _____, _____, and _____[3]. When all are working together as designed, the outcome will be _____ _____[4].

Children, obey your parents in the Lord, for this is right. "Honor your father and mother," which is the first commandment with promise: "that it may be well with you and you may live long on the earth." And you, fathers, do not provoke your children to wrath, but bring them up in the training and admonition of the Lord.

- Ephesians 6:1-4

For he is God's minister to you for good. But if you do evil, be afraid; for he does not bear the sword in vain; for he is God's minister, an avenger to execute wrath on him who practices evil.

- Romans 13:4

And He Himself gave some to be apostles, some prophets, some evangelists, and some pastors and teachers, for the equipping of the saints for the work of ministry...

- Ephesians 4:11-12

Whatever makes men good Christians, makes them good citizens.

- Daniel Webster

What does the Bible say in Genesis 1 and 2 is the duty of man? _____ _____ _____[5].

What are the 7 Mountains of cultural engagement? _____, _____, _____, _____, _____, _____, _____.[6]

The average length of a national constitution across world history is ____[7] years.

According to a University of Houston study of roughly 15,000 writings of the Founding Fathers, the most often quoted sources used by the Founding Fathers were:[ii]

4th	_____ [8]	2.9%
3rd	_____ [9]	7.9%
2nd	_____ [10]	8.3%
1st	_____ [11]	34%

Resistance to sudden violence for the preservation not only of my person, my limbs, and life, but of my property, is an indisputable right of nature which I never surrendered to the public by the compact of society and which, perhaps, I could not surrender if I would. The maxims of the law and the precepts of Christianity are precisely coincident in relation to this subject.

- John Adams

The great natural law of self-preservation cannot be repealed or superseded or suspended by any human institution. The right of the citizens to bear arms in the defense of themselves shall not be questioned. Every man's house is deemed by the law to be his castle; and the law invests him with the power and places on him the duty of the commanding officer of his house. Every man's house is his castle, and if anyone be robbed in it, it shall be esteemed his own default and negligence.

- James Wilson

Your house is your _____[12] and you are the _____
_____[13] of your house.

_____ _____[14] was considered a father to the
Founding Fathers.

He argued passionately against _____ ___
_____[15] in 1761. These documents violated a law of
nature and of nature's God which could be condensed into
Otis' summary claim that 'A man's _____[16] is his
_____[17].

*I will to my dying day oppose with all the powers and faculties
God has given me, all such instruments of slavery and villainy
as this writ of assistance is. It is the worst instrument of arbitrary
power and is destructive of liberty and the fundamental principles
of law. One of the most essential rights is the freedom of one's
house – a man's house is his castle, but these writs totally
annihilate this right. It is a power that places the liberty of every
man in the hands of every petty officer…who may reign secure
in his petty tyranny and spread terror and desolation around
him. Both reason and the Constitution are against such writs.*

- James Otis

Founding Father John Adams would later recall the
speech by James Otis in this way:

*American independence was then and there born…Every man
in the crowded audience went away, as I did, ready to take arms*

against writs of assistance. Then and there was the first scene of the first act of opposition to the arbitrary claims of Great Britain. Then and there the child Independence was born. In fifteen years, namely in 1776, he grew up to manhood and declared himself free.

- John Adams

Amendments are intended to protect _____ _____ [18] rights.

When you make a loan of any kind to your neighbor, do not go into their house to get what is offered to you as a pledge. Stay outside and let the neighbor to whom you are making the loan bring the pledge out to you.

- Deuteronomy 24:10-11

4th Amendment: The right of the people to be secure in their persons, houses, _____ [19], and effects, against unreasonable searches and seizures, shall not be violated, and no _____ [20] shall issue, but upon probable _____ [21], supported by oath or affirmation, and particularly describing the _____ [22] to be searched, and the _____ [23] or _____ [24] to be seized.

America was largely defined early on by two cities, _____ and _____ [25].

Plymouth was founded in _____ [26].

Approximately __[27] slaves were sold in Jamestown in 1619 from the British and were then hired and paid as servants.

Wentworth Cheswell was a black _____[28] official who participated in Paul Revere's midnight ride.

The _____ _____[29] started and ended as the result of two black patriots.

Charles Darwin's Origin of Species subtitle is "Preservation of _____[30] Races in the Struggle for Life."

Woodrow Wilson removed all _____[31] patriots from American history.

America was not ever a world leader in the global _____ _____[32].

America was the _____[33] nation to sign a law banning the slave trade.

Many nations today still have not passed bans on _____[34].

_____[35] million people are enslaved today.

WEEK THREE
Understanding the Times

...of the sons of Issachar who had understanding of the times, to know what Israel ought to do, their chiefs were two hundred; and all their brethren were at their command;

- 1 Chronicles 12:32

Three out of Five Americans believe there is no moral absolute _____.[1]

One out of two _____[2] believe there is no absolute moral truth.

The fastest growing forms of _____[3] in America are non-religion and anti-religion.

In 5800 years of recorded history, _____[4] has never worked once in any culture in any century.

Truth and fact have been replaced by _____ _____.[5]

They did not receive the love of the truth, that they might be saved. And for this reason God will send them strong delusion, that they should believe the lie, that they all might be condemned (damned in KJV) who did not believe the truth.

- II Thessalonians 2:10-12

_____ [6] broke out of socialism in the 1600s before any other major nation.

Believing a _____ [7] has a high cost and consequence as it always causes harm.

As people of God, we have to be lovers of _____ [8] more than anything else.

Sanctify them by the truth. Your word is truth.

- John 17:17

_____ _____ [9] is the source of absolute truth. If we're not in it, we're not going to have the truth we need. The _____ [10] addresses every issue we face.

I am the way, the truth, and the life, No one comes to the Father except through Me.

- John 14:6

Americans must now work hard to _____ [11] truth.

But as for the cowardly, the faithless, the detestable, as for murderers, the sexually immoral, sorcerers, idolaters, and all liars, their portion will be in the lake that burns with fire and sulfur, which is the second death.

- Revelation 21:8

Defending the truth requires _____.[12]

To turn the culture, we must: _____[13] the truth, _____[14] the truth, and _____[15] the truth.

It is time for us to heed the challenge of our very first Chief Justice of the U.S. Supreme Court, John Jay:

Every member of the State ought diligently to read and to study the constitution of his country, and teach the rising generation to be free. By _____ their rights, they will sooner _____ when they are violated, and be the better prepared to _____ and _____[16] them.[iii]

This quote by one of the authors of *The Federalist Papers* sums up the purpose of this class and provides the outline of our journey together through our founding documents.

It is important to spend time in the past because history shows us the _____[17] that has made us the most successful nation in history up to this point.

It's important not only to _____ [18] what is Constitutional, but also to _____ [19] our Constitutional rights. You do not win by being on defense, you win by being on offense.

The Constitution still works today, even two centuries later, because it was based on timeless _____ [20] of jurisdiction that govern human behavior.

The Founding Fathers believed that a lack of patriotism was selfishness:

Patriotism is as much a virtue as justice, and is as necessary for the support of societies as natural affection is for the support of families. The amor patriae [love of country] is both a _____ and a _____ [21] duty. It comprehends not only the love of our neighbors but of millions of our fellow creatures, not only of the present but of future generations.

- Benjamin Rush

Dr. Benjamin Rush taught that the purpose of public schools is to teach students to love and serve _____, their _____, and their _____. [22]

Dr. Rush put country before family because he understood that if we ever lost control of our country, it would become the _____ _____ [23] of our families.

Most of the Signers of the *Declaration of Independence* signed the document on _____[24]. Many of them believed it would be their _____ _____[25].

At the age of only 21, Captain _____ _____[26] was captured after volunteering for a recon mission. Just before he was hung, he gave a passionate speech for freedom and closed with his famous "one life" statement that has inspired generations to sacrifice for freedom.

No greater love has any man than that he lay down his life for his friends.   **- John 15:13**

The best way to honor those who gave their one life for our freedom is to _____[27] the freedom that they sacrificed their lives for, as Captain Miller said in *Saving Private Ryan*.

Abraham Lincoln said we should take "_____ _____[28] *to the cause for which they gave the last full measure of devotion.*" [iv]

THE FATE OF THE FREE WORLD DEPENDS UPON _____[29]!

Help prepare the next generation by getting your local school district to participate in _____ _____ _____[30]. (visit PatriotAcademy.com/CFW and click on your state to see how you can help.)

Our Approach to Study of the Constitution

1. This is not an exhaustive Constitutional study.

Think of this class as the "_____ _____ _____[31]" to the Constitution, so we as citizens can get plugged in. Then, you should go back home and study the Constitution more extensively.

Recommended resources for further study:

o The Full 10-Week *Constitution Alive!* Series (PatriotAcademy.com)

o The Full *Foundations of Freedom* Series (WallBuilders.com)

o *The 5,000-Year Leap* by W. Cleon Skousen

o *The Heritage Guide to the Constitution* by Edwin Meese, Dr. Matthew Spalding, and Dr. David Forte

o *Constitutional Literacy* with Mike Farris

o Stansbury's *Catechism on the Constitution* (PatriotAcademy.com)

Our goal is to _____ our rights, and know how to _____ and _____[32] them.

2. Focus on _____ _____[33], not judicial interpretation.

On every question of construction, carry ourselves back to the time when the Constitution was adopted, recollect the spirit manifested in the debates, and instead of trying what meaning may be squeezed out of the text, or invented against it, conform to the probable one in which it was passed.[v]

- Thomas Jefferson

I entirely concur in the propriety of resorting to the sense in which the Constitution was accepted and ratified by the nation. In that sense alone it is the legitimate Constitution. And if that be not the guide in expounding it, there can be no security for a consistent and stable [constitution], more than for a faithful, exercise of its powers.

- James Madison

What a metamorphosis would be produced in the code of law if all its ancient phraseology were to be taken in its modern sense.

- James Madison

The first and governing maxim in the interpretation of a statute is to discover the meaning of those who made it.

- James Wilson

The first and fundamental rule in the interpretation of all documents is to construe them according to the sense of the terms and the intentions of the parties.[vi]

- Joseph Story

3. Take sections as _____[34].

4. Use plain language for basic understanding,
   but not a substitute for the _____ _____[35].

In Appendix E of this workbook, you will find *The Constitution Made Easy* by Michael Holler. This has the original text on the left and the plain-language amended version on the right.

_____ _____[36] is like the "owner's manual" of the Constitution: it helps us identify the correct application of the tools we have been given.

Once we understand the original meaning, the _____[37] that is communicated is the same and completely applicable to today.

We have a responsibility to teach the Constitution, not just to the rising generation, but to _____[38] around us. In our day of social media, everyone has a _____[39].

You do not have to be super _____[40] to understand the Constitution. The founding fathers were ordinary men, and the Constitution they made was for us ordinary people.

WEEK FOUR
The Seeds of Liberty

*[T]he virtue which had been infused into the Constitution of the United States ... was no other than the concretion of those abstract principles which had been first proclaimed in the Declaration of Independence.... **This was the platform upon which the Constitution of the United States had been erected.** Its virtues, its republican character, consisted in its conformity to the principles proclaimed in the Declaration of Independence and as its administration ... was to depend upon the ... virtue, or in other words, of those principles proclaimed in the Declaration of Independence and embodied in the Constitution of the United States.*[vii]

- **John Quincy Adams, at "The Jubilee of the Constitution"**

In business terms, the Declaration of Independence is like the _____ of _____[1], telling who we are and what we are about, and the Constitution is like the _____[2], telling how the business will operate.

Before the formation of the Constitution, the Declaration was received and ratified by all the States in the Union and has never been disannulled.[viii]

- Samuel Adams, Father of the American Revolution

[The Constitution] is but the body and the letter of which the former is the thought and the spirit, and it is always safe to read the letter of the Constitution in the spirit of the Declaration of Independence.[ix]

- U.S. Supreme Court

The Framers' Formula for Lasting Freedom

*We hold these **truths to be self-evident**: that all men are created equal, that they are **endowed by their Creator** with certain unalienable rights, that among these are life, liberty, and the **pursuit of happiness**; that to secure these rights, governments are instituted among men, deriving their just powers from the **consent of the governed...**[x]*

The Declaration of Independence includes four essential principles that hold our freedom firmly in place:

1. _____[3] (The undeniable fact that moral absolutes exist.)

2. _____[4] (Our unalienable right to individual freedom comes from God)

3. _____[5] (We have a voice in our government.)

4. _____[6] (The importance of free enterprise to our freedom.)

Self-evident Truths & Endowed by Our Creator

Of all the dispositions and habits which lead to political prosperity, religion and morality are indispensable supports. In vain would that man claim the tribute of patriotism, who should labor to subvert these great pillars of human happiness.... The mere politician, equally with the pious man, ought to respect and to cherish them.[xi]

- George Washington

The American Revolution was _____ _____ _____[7] and it led to the most successful nation in the history of the world. The French Revolution was _____ _____ _____[8] and it led to the guillotine and total chaos.

The normal model of government in 1776 was based on the idea that power flowed from _____ to the _____ to the _____[9].

The American model of government reversed the last two so that power flows from _____ directly to _____ and then power is given to _____[10] only as the people deem appropriate.

If government does not _____[11] us our freedom, then government cannot rightfully _____[12] it away.

Thomas Jefferson even noted that the firm _____ ____ _____[13] was for people to remember that liberty is a gift from God.[xii]

When delegates to the Constitutional Convention began to despair, _____[14] Franklin, the elder statesman, spoke on June 28, 1787, in an attempt to get the delegates back on track.

Mr. President, the small progress we have made after four or five weeks close attendance & continual reasonings with each other— our different sentiments on almost every question, several of the last producing as many noes and ayes, is methinks a melancholy proof of the imperfection of the Human Understanding. We indeed seem to feel our own want of political wisdom, since we have been running about in search of it. We have gone back to ancient history for models of Government, and examined the different forms of those Republics which having been formed with the seeds of their own dissolution now no longer exist. And we have viewed Modern States all round Europe, but find none of their Constitutions suitable to our circumstances.

"In this situation of this Assembly, groping as it were in the dark to find political truth, and scarce able to distinguish it when presented to us, how has it happened, Sir, that we have not hitherto once thought of humbly applying to the Father of lights to illuminate our understandings?

In the beginning of the contest with Great Britain, when we were sensible to danger, we had daily prayer in this room for Divine protection. Our prayers, Sir, were heard, and they were graciously answered. All of us who were engaged in the struggle must have observed frequent instances of a superintending Providence in our favor... [H]ave we now forgotten that powerful Friend? Or do we imagine we no longer need His assistance? I have lived, Sir, a long time, and the longer I live, the more convincing proofs I see of this truth—that God governs in the affairs of men. And if a sparrow cannot fall to the ground without His notice, is it probable that an empire can rise without His aid?

We have been assured, Sir, in the Sacred Writing, that 'except the Lord build the House, they labor in vain that build it.' I firmly believe this; and I also believe that without His concurring aid we shall succeed in this political building no better than the builders of Babel...

I therefore beg leave to move—that henceforth prayers imploring the assistance of Heaven, and its blessing on our deliberations, be held in this Assembly every morning before we proceed to business... [xiii]

- Benjamin Franklin, Declaration and Constitution Signer

The real wonder is that the Constitutional Convention overcame so many difficulties. And to overcome them with so much agreement was as unprecedented as it was unexpected. It is impossible for the pious man not to recognize in it a finger of that Almighty Hand which was so frequently extended to us in the critical stages of the Revolution.[xiv]

- James Madison, Father of the Constitution

For my own part, I sincerely esteem a system which, without the finger of God, never could have been suggested and agreed upon by such a diversity of interests.[xv]

- Alexander Hamilton, Constitution Signer & co-author of the Federalist Papers

As to my sentiments with respect to the new Constitution, it appears to me little short of a miracle. It demonstrates as visibly the finger of Providence as any possible event in the course of human affairs can ever designate it.[xvi]

- George Washington, Constitution Signer & Presiding Officer of the Convention

The Pursuit of Happiness

A wise and frugal government, which shall leave men free to regulate their own pursuits of industry and improvement, and shall not take from the mouth of labor bread it has earned - this is the sum of good government.[xvii]   **- Thomas Jefferson**

William Bradford and the Pilgrims tried socialism, which Governor Bradford said caused much "_____ and _____[15], *and retard[ed] much employment, that would have been to their benefit, and comfort"*[xviii] and caused people to *"allege weakness and inability."*

After starving literally to death (many of them), Bradford made two very important changes by implementing _____   _____ and _____ _____[16].

They were soon exporting corn and thriving.

This had very good success; for it made all hands very industrious, so as much more corn was planted, than otherwise would have been; by any means the Governor or any other could use, and saved him a great deal of trouble, and gave far better content.[xix]

- Gov. William Bradford

NOTE: Remember all this when we get to the Commerce Clause in Article 1, Section 8!

(Be sure to enjoy the bonus videos found in your free digital version of this workbook at BiblicalCitizens.com)

Consent of the Governed

It is a great mistake to suppose that the paper we are to propose will govern the United States. It is the men whom it will bring into the Government and interest in maintaining it that is to govern them. The paper will only mark out the mode and the form. Men are the substance and must do the business.[xx]

**- John Francis Mercer, delegate
to the Constitutional Convention**

If we want to uphold the Constitution, we have to make _____ _____[17] in choosing our leaders, be part of the process, and be engaged in our government.

In our final class, we will discuss the proper, constitutional way to fulfill our duty in giving or refusing our consent.

The Six Immutable Principles in the Declaration of Independence:

1. There is a divine _____[18].

Believing in a divine Creator is the first step toward _____ _____[19], because if government is all-supreme, there is nothing that can impose limits.

If God is not in the national equation, then _____[20] becomes god.

2. _____ _____ [21] **come from God.**

Every person has a set of _____ [22] given by the Creator, not government, which government has no _____ [23] to interfere with.

3. **Government exists to _____ [24] inalienable rights.**

Government is not there to _____ [25] for us, but to protect us while we go out and produce. The more government provides for us, the less _____ [26] we are because the less initiative we have.

4. **There is a _____ _____ [27] law.**

A lack of a fixed moral law leads to _____ [28], where every person gets to decide for themselves what is right and wrong and the powerful control the weak. John Quincy Adams called this "the law of the tiger and the shark."

5. **The _____ [29] of the governed, or the will of the majority.**

This principle only follows the principles stating that there are inalienable _____ [30] and a fixed _____ _____ [31]. The consent of the governed does not overrule these basic truths.

6. **The people's right to ____ their _____**[32].

Because government comes _____ ____ _____[33], we can change our government in any way needed if the first five principles are violated.

Richard Henry Lee said that Thomas Jefferson "_____[34]" the Declaration of Independence from John Locke's book "The Two Treatises of Government," which cites the Bible over _____[35] times to show the proper operation of civil government.

Every right set forth in the Declaration had been _____[36] from the American _____[37] prior to 1763.

Many phrases in the Declaration of Independence were originally preached by Rev. _____ _____[38] whose sermons were reprinted and published by the founding fathers before the Revolution.

In George Washington's day, "duty" meant a _____ _____[39] contractual obligation.

It is the duty of all nations to acknowledge the Providence of Almighty God, to obey His will, to be grateful for His benefits, and humbly to implore His protection and favor.

- George Washington

Assignments:

In your own words, why is it important to study the *Declaration of Independence* in a class on the *Constitution?*

_____

_____

_____

_____

Using the full text of both documents in Appendix C and E of this book, compare *Declaration* grievance #3 to Article 1, Section 2 of the *Constitution.* Then find the Clause in the *Constitution* that is connected to the following Grievances in the *Declaration*:

Grievance #4: Article 1, Section 5, Clause _____ [40]

Grievance #5: Article 1, Section 4, Clause _____ [41]

Grievance #7: Article 1, Section _____ [42] **, Clause 4**

Grievance #8: Article ____ [43] **, Section 8, Clause 9**

Grievance #11: Article 1, Section ___, Clause ___ [44]

Grievance #12: Article ___, Section ___, Clause ___ [45]

Grievance #14: The _____ [46] **Amendment**

Grievance #18: The _____ and _____ [47] **Amendments**

As I have traveled across the country, I have been astounded just how many of our fellow citizens feel strongly about their constitutional rights but have no idea what they are, or for that matter, what the Constitution says. I am not suggesting that they become Constitutional scholars -- whatever that means. I am suggesting, however, that if one feels strongly about his or her rights, it does make sense to know generally what the Constitution says about them. It is at least as easy to understand as a cell phone contract -- and vastly more important.[xxi]

- Clarence Thomas, U.S. Supreme Court Justice

We the people of the United States, in order to form a more perfect Union, establish justice, insure domestic tranquility, provide for the common defense, promote the general welfare, and secure the blessings of liberty to ourselves and our posterity, do ordain and establish this Constitution for the United States of America.

- Preamble to the Constitution

General Welfare: *Exemption from any unusual evil or calamity; the enjoyment of peace and prosperity, or the ordinary blessings of society and civil government; applied to states.* (emphasis added)

- Webster's 1828 Dictionary

"General welfare" is not "_____ _____[48];" it only applies to the states and the system in general.

If not from _____[49], where do the *Blessings of liberty*' come from?

The _____[50] Amendment limited any person to serve as president to no more than two full terms, thereby curbing the power of the executive branch. This was ratified after _____ _____ _____[51] was elected to a fourth presidential term, and the American people had decided that was too long and too much power.

The District of Columbia was designed by Article 1, Section 8, Paragraph 17 not to be a _____[52] or within a _____[53], but rather a special place for the seat of the federal government.

The 23rd Amendment gives citizens in D.C. the right to _____ for _____[54] by granting D.C. the same number of electors in the electoral college as the smallest state.

*The 1800 rematch election between Adams and Jefferson also created confusion when the old process created a tie in the electoral college between Jefferson and his running mate Aaron Burr due to there being no distinction between electoral votes cast for President or Vice-President. The tie threw the election to Congress, which finally chose Jefferson after several dozen ballots.

U.S. CONSTITUTION AT A GLANCE

ARTICLES

I   = _____ 55
II   = _____ 56
III = _____ 57
IV   = _____ 58
V   = _____ 59
VI   = _____ 60
VII = _____ 61

AMENDMENTS

1-10   = _____ 62
12*, 20, 22, 23, 25   = _____ 63
11   = _____ 64
17, 20, 27   = _____ 65
13, 14, 15   = _____ 66
15, 19, 24, 26   = _____ 67
16   = _____ 68
18, 21   = _____ 69

BILL OF RIGHTS

1st = _____ 70
2nd = _____ 71
3rd = _____ 72
4th = _____ 73
5th = _____ 74
6th = _____ 75
7th = _____ 76
8th = _____ 77
9th = _____ 78
10th = _____ 79

NOTE: The filled in *Constitution At a Glance* are in Appendix A

The _____[80] Amendment changed the way
_____[81] are elected, removing the check and
balance of states' ability to curb federal encroachment
upon state jurisdictions.

The 14th Amendment _____[82] the
Constitution to the states, not just the Federal
government.

For a detailed description of the history of the 14th
Amendment, read Justice Clarence Thomas' Concurring
Opinion in McDonald v. Chicago and his argument for
why the 14th guarantees all citizens the same privileges and
immunities. You can view the opinion online here:

http://www.law.cornell.edu/supct/html/08-1521.ZC1.html

The "voting" amendments were significant because
the majority was giving the _____[83] the ability to
_____[84], which is rarely seen in other countries.

The _____[85] Amendment was necessary for
Congress to ban alcohol because the people had never
given them, through the Constitution, the authority to do
so.

****

WEEK FIVE
Who Has Authority?

Render unto Caesar that which is Caesar's, and unto God that which is God's. **- Matthew 22:21**

A _____ _____[1] is one that recognizes jurisdictional lines – to understand what belongs to government and what does not, not one that is necessarily small in size.

Marriage is part of the _____ _____[2]; therefore God is the one Who defines it. Government cannot cross that _____[3] line and change it to be something else.

Government has jurisdiction to _____ and _____[4] marriage as defined by God.

Texas Supreme Court in Grigsby v. Reid, 1913

Marriage was not originated by human law. When God created Eve, she was a wife to Adam; they then and there occupied the status of husband to wife and wife to husband. The truth is that civil government has grown out of marriage, which created homes and population and society, from which government became necessary.

Marriages will produce a home and family that will contribute to good society, to free and just government, and the support of Christianity.

It would be sacrilegious to apply the designation "a civil contract" to such a marriage. It is that and more – it is a status ordained by God.

The founding fathers said that the "general welfare" clause was not to be interpreted as saying an industry was too ____ ___ _____[5] and needs a bailout, during the debates concerning bailing out the codfish industry in 1791.

_____

_____

_____

_____

If Congress can employ money indefinitely to the general welfare, and are the sole and supreme judges of the general welfare, they may take the care of religion into their own hands; they may appoint teachers in every State, county and parish and pay them out of their public treasury; they may take into their own hands the education of children, establishing in like manner schools throughout the Union; they may assume the provision of the poor; they may undertake the regulation of all roads other than post-roads; in short, every thing, from the highest object of state legislation down to the most minute object of police, would be thrown under the power of Congress. ... Were the power of Congress to be established in the latitude contended for, it would subvert the very foundations, and transmute the very nature of the limited Government established by the people of America.

- James Madison

- **Section 8 of the Constitution contains DO's for the _____ _____** [6]

- **Section 9 of the Constitution contains DON'Ts for the _____ _____** [7]

- **Section 10 of the Constitution contains DON'Ts for the _____** [8]

Congress cannot add power ___ _____[9]; it only comes from us.

Congress has the power to collect taxes for these purposes:

- To pay the _____[10]
- To provide for the common _____[11] and general _____[12] of the United States

The Founders believed that to carry debt over to the next generation is _____[13].

Hamilton said that the test for spending money Constitutionally is whether it is for a _____[14] purpose or a _____[15] purpose.

The welfare of the community (of states) is the only legitimate end for which money can be raised from the community. Congress can be considered as only under one restriction, which does not apply to other governments. They cannot rightfully apply the money they raise to any purpose merely or purely local... The constitutional test of a right application must always be whether it be for a purpose of general or local nature.

- Alexander Hamilton

Consider for a moment the immeasurable difference between the Constitution limited in its powers to the enumerated objects, and expounded as it would be by the import claimed for the phraseology in question.

The difference is equivalent to two Constitutions, of characters essentially contrasted with each other--the one possessing powers confined to certain specified cases, the other extended to all cases whatsoever;...

Can less be said...than that it is impossible that such a Constitution as the latter would have been recommended to the States by all the members of that body whose names were subscribed to the instrument? ... Is it credible that such a power would have been unnoticed and unopposed in the Federal Convention? In the State Conventions, which contended for, and proposed restrictive and explanatory amendments? And in the Congress of 1789, which recommended so many of these amendments? A power to impose unlimited taxes for unlimited purposes could never have escaped...those public bodies.

Constitution is a limited one, possessing no power not actually given, and carrying on the face of it a distrust of power beyond the distrust indicated by the ordinary forms of free Government.[xxii]

- James Madison

A balanced budget amendment to the Constitution failed in 1999 by how many votes? _____[16]

"Regulate commerce" means "make _____[17]," not "micromanage."

Congress has the power to regulate commerce:

- with _____[18] nations
- Between the several _____[19]
- With the _____ _____[20]

This was not a license to _____-_____[21] the market.

Jefferson said that "The pillars of our prosperity are the most thriving when left most free to _____ _____[22]."

The Founders were specific about everything in the Constitution because they had a real _____ of _____[23].

Our system has separation of powers between the
_____ of _____[24] as well as the branches.

*Nothing is more certain, than that the forms of liberty may
be retained, when the substance is gone. In government, as well
as in religion, 'The letter killeth, but the spirit giveth life.'*

- John Dickinson, Constitution Signer

It is important to follow the _____[25] of the
"general welfare" clause and the rest of the Constitution,
rather than trying to squeeze a new meaning out of the
wording.

*Shall we establish nothing good because we know it cannot
be eternal? Shall we live without government because every
constitution has its old age and its period? Because we know
that we shall die, shall we take no pains to preserve or
lengthen our life?*

*Far from it, Sir: it only requires the more watchful attention
to settle government upon the best principles and in the wisest
manner that it may last as long as the nature of things will
permit.*

- John Witherspoon

Samuel Adams stated that the man who conscientiously does his duty will be protected by God and receive an _____ _____ [26].

In having secured the approval of our hearts by a faithful and unwearied discharge of our <u>duty</u> to our country let us joyfully leave our concerns in the hands of Him Who raises up and pulls down the empires and kingdoms of the world as He pleases.

- John Hancock

All that the best men can do is to persevere in doing their duty to their country and leave the consequences to Him Who made it their duty, being neither elated by success, however great, nor discouraged by disappointment, however frequent and mortifying.

We must go home to be happy, and our home is not in this world. Here we have nothing to do but our duty, and by it to regulate our business and our pleasure.

- John Jay, first Supreme Court Chief Justice

Currently, in city and school board elections, only _____ [27] of Americans show up to vote.

Nations get healthy from the _____ _____ [28], not the top down.

WEEK SIX
Of Kings and Courts

THE PRESIDENCY OF THE UNITED STATES

In an _____ _____ _____[1] delivered to the new Connecticut government by **Rev. Matthias Burnett**, he said:

> *To God and posterity you are accountable for [your rights and your rulers]...Let not your children have reason to curse you for giving up those rights, and prostrating those institutions which our fathers delivered to you as a sacred palladium, and which by the blessing of God have been peculiarly beneficial to the order, peace and prosperity of this State...*

The most significant part of the President's responsibilities is to make sure the laws are _____ _____[2].

John Adams said that faithfully executing the laws would make us a nation of _____[3] and not of _____[4].

The interest of the people is one thing: it is the public interest. And where the public interest governs, it is a government of laws and not of men.

The interest of a king or of a party is another thing: it is a private interest. And where private interest governs, it is a nation of men and not of laws.   **- John Adams**

In public officials, look for people who will set _____ _____[5] and enforce the will of the people.

The _____[6], more than any other entity, is the one who decides whether we are a government of laws or a government of men.

The Electoral College is a way for the _____[7] to have a voice, and the _____[8] to have a voice in the election of the President.

The Founders rejected having the President elected by _____ _____[9] because the most populated areas would outvote the more rural areas.

The Founding Fathers used the Electoral College to strike a balance that would require the winner to have both a _____ _____[10] of the people AND a sufficient _____[11] of the vote.

In a popular vote scenario, the major deciders for the Presidency would be the _____ _____[12].

I view great cities as pestilential to the morals, the health, and the liberties of man.

- Thomas Jefferson, writing to Benjamin Rush

I agree with you in your opinion of cities. Cowper the poet very happily expresses our ideas of them compared with the country. 'God made the country; man made cities.' I consider them in the same light that I do abscesses on the human body – as reservoirs of all the impurities of a community.

- Benjamin Rush, writing back to Jefferson

Supporters of National Popular Vote want _____ _____[13], rather than a constitutional republic.

Pure democracy cannot subsist long nor be carried far into the departments of state – it is very subject to caprice and the madness of popular rage.

- John Witherspoon, Signer of the Declaration of Independence

Remember, democracy never lasts long. It soon wastes, exhausts, and murders itself. There never was a democracy yet that did not commit suicide."[xxiii]   **- John Adams**

A simple democracy is one of the greatest of evils. A democracy is a mobocracy.[xxiv]

- Benjamin Rush, Signer of the Declaration

Section _____[14] of the 25th Amendment is the process by which the President declares he/she is unable to fulfill the duties of the presidency.

Section _____[15] of the 25th Amendment is the process by which the VP and a majority of the Cabinet declare the President unable to fulfill the duties of the presidency.

When has the 25th Amendment been invoked under Section 4? _____ [16].

At the time of this recording, the only time the 25th Amendment was invoked under Section 3 was once by President _____[17] and twice by President _____[18].

The practice of issuing Executive Orders started with President _____ [19].

Executive Orders are Constitutional if they are executing a law that _____ [20] has actually _____ [21].

The Founders believed that the foundation of oaths was in being more _____ of _____ [22] than of following the oath.

The 1776 Pennsylvania Constitution written by Benjamin Franklin barred anyone from holding office unless they believed in "a future state of _____ and _____ [23]."

If the president alone was vested with the power of appointing all officers, and was left to select a council for himself, he would be liable to be deceived by flatterers and pretenders to patriotism, who would have no motive but their own emolument [self-seeking profit and gain].

- Roger Sherman, Declaration of Independence and Constitution Signer

_____

_____

_____

THE JUDICIARY OF THE UNITED STATES

If you believe in _____[24] as a philosophy of life, it permeates every area, including your view of the Constitution.

Today, the law schools teach that judges are responsible for ____ _____[25].

Of the 27 grievances in the Declaration of Independence, ___[26] of them were regarding judges.

The Founders wanted to avoid _____[27] appointments for judges.

Law schools don't teach truth ___ ___ _____[28], they teach "truth" ___ _____ _____ ___ ___ ____[29], which leaves them in charge of what happens to the Constitution.

The judicial branch has _____ _____[30] they were never designed to have because we the people have not known the Constitution ourselves.

Samuel Adams complained about judicial tyranny in the form of _____ ___ _____[31] and _____ _____[32] as far back as 1765.

Myth #1: The three branches are co-equal.

The Federalist Papers were written by _____, _____, and _____[33] and are like an instruction manual for the Constitution.

In Federalist Paper 51, Madison said the _____[34] branch "necessarily predominates" because it is the branch that is _____ to the _____[35].

In Federalist Paper 78, Hamilton said the _____[36] was the weakest branch and would not be a threat to our liberty if it remained in its proper jurisdiction.

> ...the judiciary is beyond comparison the weakest of the three departments of power; ...the general liberty of the people can never be endangered from that quarter; I mean so long as the judiciary remains truly distinct from both the legislature and the Executive... And it proves, in the last place, that as

liberty can have nothing to fear from the judiciary alone, but would have every thing to fear from its union with either of the other departments; The judiciary... has no influence over either the sword or the purse; no direction either of the strength or of the wealth of the society; and can take no active resolution whatever. It may truly be said to have neither force nor will, but merely judgment; and must ultimately depend upon the aid of the executive arm even for the efficacy of its judgments.

- Alexander Hamilton, Federalist 78

The judiciary was established by and is accountable to the other _____ _____[37] of government, because they owe a _____[38] to the people.

Superficial observers take it for granted that the three departments of government are co-ordinate and independent of each other. It is to be observed that the words 'co-ordinate,' 'independent,' are not to be found in any part of the Constitution. According to the Constitution, the establishment of the Judiciary department was entrusted to the Legislative department. Is the Judiciary department formed by the Constitution? It is not. It is only declared that there shall be such a department, and it is directed to be formed by the other two departments, who owe a responsibility to the people. The number of judges, the affirmation of duties, the fixing of compensations, the fixing the times when, and the places where, the courts shall exercise the functions, &c., are left to the entire discretion of Congress. Congress may postpone the sessions of the courts for eight to ten years and establish others to whom they could transfer all the powers of the existing courts. The spirit, as well as the words of the Constitution, are completely satisfied, provided one Supreme Court be established.

- William Giles

The Constitution leaves it entirely to the discretion of _____ [39] as to how many members will be on the court and how many lower courts to establish from time to time.

Congress may also set the _____ [40], removing issues from the purview of the court.

The provision of the act of 1867, affirming the appellate jurisdiction of this court in cases of habeas corpus is expressly repealed. It is hardly possible to imagine a plainer instance of positive exception. We are not at liberty to inquire into the motives of the legislature. We can only examine into its power under the Constitution; and the power to make exceptions to the appellate jurisdiction of this court is given by express words. Without jurisdiction the court cannot proceed at all in any cause... It is quite clear, therefore, that

*this court cannot proceed to pronounce judgment in this case,
for it has no longer jurisdiction of the appeal; and judicial
duty is not less fitly performed by declining ungranted
jurisdiction than in exercising firmly that which the
Constitution and the laws confer.*

- U.S. Supreme Court in *Ex Parte McCardle*[xxv]

Myth #2: Federal judges hold lifetime appointments.

Judges are *not* appointed for life, they are appointed
for _____ _____[41].

*The judges both of the Supreme and inferior courts, shall hold
their offices during good behavior.*

- Article III, Sec. 1

*We all fully and at once understand what is 'good behavior'
in a judge, and if he acts contrary, it would be misbehavior;
and the Constitution in that case has given a remedy by
impeachment.*

- John Calhoun

The House of Representatives has the power to
impeach *(essentially an indictment, not a finding of guilt or
innocence)* and the Senate has the sole power to _____[42]
all impeachments.

Judges have been impeached for:

- Issuing an order _____ [43] an act of Congress
- Drunkenness in private life
- _____ [44] in the courtroom
- Profanity
- Judicial _____-_____ [45]

According to Hamilton, impeachment is a _____ [46] in the hands of the legislature.

Each branch is furnished with constitutional arms for its own effectual powers of self-defense.

- Alexander Hamilton

Every government requires impeachment. Every man ought to be accountable for his conduct... Impeachment will be not only a means of punishing misconduct but will also prevent misconduct. A man in public office who knows that there is no tribunal to punish him may be ready to deviate from his duty; but if he knows there is a tribunal for that purpose, although he may be a man of no principle, the very terror of punishment will perhaps deter him.

- James Iredell

...all powers residing originally in the people and being derived from them, the several magistrate and officers of government vested with authority – whether legislative, executive, or judicial – are their substitutes and agents and are at all times accountable to them.

- Sam Adams, John Hancock, John Adams in the Massachusetts State Constitution

Here, the people are masters of government; elsewhere, the government is master of the people.

- James Wilson

To review the other myths of the judiciary, take the full ***Constitution Alive!*** course at PatriotAcademy.com.

WEEK SEVEN
Religious Liberty

The purpose of government is to secure
_____ _____[1], which is the function of
the Bill of Rights.

Signer of the Constitution John Dickinson defined
an inalienable right as a right "which God gave to you and
no inferior power has a right to _____ _____[2]."

*[Human governments] could not give the rights essential to
happiness… We claim them from a higher source – from
the King of kings and Lord of all the earth. They are not
annexed to us by parchments and seals. They are created in
us by the decrees of Providence, which establish the laws of
our nature. They are born with us; exist with us; and cannot
be taken from us by any human power, without taking our
lives.*

- John Dickinson, Constitution Signer

Inalienable rights are:

not to be rummaged for, among old parchments, or musty records. They are written, as with a sun beam, in the whole volume of human nature, by the hand of the divinity itself; and can never be erased or obscured by mortal power."
- Alexander Hamilton, Constitution Signer & co-author of the Federalist Papers

imprinted by the finger of God on the heart of man.
- Samuel Adams, Signer of the Declaration

antecedent to all earthly government; rights that cannot be repealed or restrained by human law; rights derived from the great Legislator of the Universe.
- John Adams, Signer of the Declaration

The Noahide laws, the first earthly government established by God, were given to _____ _____ _____ [3].

Our nation has only fallen by _____ _____ [4]: our government has forgotten that there is a Power higher than itself.

The five fundamental freedoms in the First Amendment are: _____, _____, _____, _____, _____, & _____ [5].

Congress shall make no law respecting an establishment of religion, or prohibiting the free exercise thereof. . . .[xxvi]

Where in the Constitution is the phrase *"separation of church and state?"* _____ [6]

To understand the "intent" of the legislators who pass any law, one must look at the _____ [7] where the discussions that took place at the time the law was being debated were recorded.

Article _____, Section _____[8] of the *Constitution* requires that everything said on the floor of the House and Senate be recorded in a journal.[xxvii]

How many times do the Annals of Congress record the phrase *"separation of church and state"* during the debates drafting the First Amendment? _____ [9]

The phrase appears in a letter from _____ _____ [10] to the Danbury Baptists, assuring them that government would not _____[11] on their freedom of religion.

James Madison said that the intent of the First Amendment was to prevent a _____ _____ _____ [12], like the Church of England.

Two days after writing the phrase *"separation of church and state,"* Thomas Jefferson attended the weekly church service held at _____ [13]. These were religious services that he had helped to start and faithfully attended throughout the remainder of his presidency.[xxviii]

General Henry Knox & Charles Thomson both wrote in their journals about accidentally interrupting George Washington _____ ___ _____ [14].

What words are usually left out of Patrick Henry's famous speech by modern historians? "_____ ___, _____ _____ [15]!"

_____ _____ [16] founded the University of Georgia and served as a _____ [17] in the Revolutionary War.

Framers of the Constitution, Charles Cotesworth Pinckney and John Langdon, were founders of the _____ _____ _____ [18].

_____ _____ _____ [19] quoted from the book of Acts to challenge public school graduates to fulfill their duties to serve their Creator and country.

Constitution Framer James McHenry helped found the _____ _____ _____ [20].

The most active and influential man of the Constitutional Convention and author of the Preamble was _____ _____[21].

Religion is the only solid basis of good morals. Therefore, education should teach the precepts of religion and the duties of man toward God.[xxix] - **Gouverneur Morris, Signer of the Constitution**

The Northwest Ordinance required public schools to teach _____, _____[22], and knowledge.[xxx]

_____ _____[23] signed both the Declaration & Constitution, and served on the original Supreme Court.

Human law must rest its authority ultimately upon the authority of that law which is divine. Far from being rivals or enemies, religion and law are twin sisters, friends, and mutual assistants. Indeed, these two sciences run into each other.[xxxi]

- James Wilson, Signer of the Constitution

If the First Amendment is reduced to "freedom of _____[24]" instead of "freedom of _____[25]," there will be no protection of conscience anymore.

James Madison called conscience "the most sacred of _____[26]."

We should be very cautious of violating the rights of conscience in others, ever considering that God alone is the judge of the hearts of men and to Him only they are answerable.

- George Washington

For what business, in the name of common sense, has the magistrate with our religion? The state does not have any concern in the matter. In what manner does it affect society in what outward form we think it best to pay our adoration to God? The consciences of men are not the objects of human legislation. In contrast with this spiritual tyranny, how beautiful appears our constitution in disclaiming all jurisdiction over the souls of men, securing by a never-to-be-repealed section the voluntary, unchecked moral persuasion of every person by his own self-directed communication with the Father of spirits!

- William Livingston, Constitution Signer

Security under our constitution is given to the rights of conscience and private judgment. They are by nature subject to no control but that of Deity, and in that free situation they are now left.

- John Jay, first Supreme Court Chief Justice

Starting in _____[27], the top issue that brought people to America was the rights of conscience.

The phrase *"the laws of nature and nature's God"* came from _____ _____ _____ _____ _____[28].

Blackstone taught that God _____ _____[29] in nature and in His laws, i.e. the holy _____[30].

The abolitionist Founding Fathers fought slavery on the basis of the laws of nature.

The Bill of Rights prohibits government from _____[31] inalienable rights and commands government to _____[32] them.

... select from all the people able men ... to be rulers of thousands, rulers of hundreds, rulers of fifties, and rulers of tens.   **- Exodus 18:21**

For the lips of a priest should keep knowledge, and the people should seek the law from his mouth...   **- Malachi 2:7**

Resistance to sudden violence for the preservation not only of my person, my limbs, and life, but of my property, is an indisputable right of nature which I never surrendered to the public by the compact of society and which, perhaps, I could not surrender if I would.... [T]he maxims of the law and the precepts of Christianity are precisely coincident in relation to this subject.[xxxii]

- John Adams, Signer of The Declaration

[T]o preserve liberty, it is essential that the whole body of the people always possess arms, and be taught alike, especially when young, how to use them…

- Richard Henry Lee, Declaration Signer

George Mason did not sign the Constitution because it did not _____ _____[33], and because he wanted more _____[34] placed around government.

The Supreme Court changed the "eminent domain" clause in the Constitution from "_____ _____[35]" to "_____ _____[36]" which makes it much easier to take private property.

Government is instituted to protect property. This being the end of government, that alone is a just government which impartially secures to every man whatever is his own. It is not a just government, nor is property secure under it, where arbitrary restrictions deny to part of its citizens that free use of their faculties or where the property which a man has in his personal safety and personal liberty is violated by arbitrary seizures of one class of citizens for the service of the rest.

- James Madison

WEEK EIGHT
Being Salt and Light

Federal law stipulates that every _Student_ _in_ [1], public schools take time to read and study the Constitution, but _90_ [2] of public schools do not do it.

You can be an _ambassador_ [3] for the Constitution in your local school district!

We need to start applying the principle of _____ [4] as we work to bring America back to her roots.

To influence ARTICLES 1 & 2:

_____! [5] The first place in the Constitution a citizen is given responsibility is the word _Chosen_ [6] in Article 1, Section 2.

Rick lost his first race by only _20_ [7] votes out of over 30,000, then won on the recount by _36_ [8] votes.

The 2000 Presidential election was determined by a mere _537_ [9] votes in Florida.

Let it be impressed on your mind that God commands you to choose for rulers just men who will rule in the fear of God.... [I]f the citizens neglect their duty and place unprincipled men in office, the government will soon be corrupted ... If [our] government fails to secure public prosperity and happiness, it must be because the citizens neglect the Divine commands, and elect bad men to make and administer the laws.[xxxiii]

- Noah Webster

The right to choose our _rulers_ *leaders* [10] is something most people in the history of the world never got to do!

When the righteous rule, the people rejoice; when the wicked rule, the people groan.

- Proverbs 29:2

The Three Ingredients In The "Mixing Bowl" Of The American System:

1. Knowledge of the people – before we can choose wisely at the polls, we must know the _plum line_ [11] by which to measure the candidates.

2. The pool of _Candidates_ [12] – find good people with leadership skills and ask them to run!

3. The _action_ [13] **of the citizens** – impact the political process by knocking on doors, making phone calls, contributing, etc.

A _political_ [14] is only thinking about the next election. A _patriot_ [15] is concerned about the next generation!

To influence ARTICLE 3:

- Influence who the _US senators_ [16] are who approve justices

- Get involved with the _federal_ [17] judiciary

- _____ [18] legal organizations like Liberty Counsel, First Liberty Institute, the Alliance Defending Freedom, ACLJ, Pacific Justice Institute, etc.

To influence ARTICLE 4:

- Educate people on how we are a _republic_ [19], not a democracy.

More ideas:

- Adopt a potential _____[20] to the Constitution as your project

- Watch out for treaties: keep up with them and call your Senators when necessary

- _Live_ [21] the Bill of Rights!

- BE the press!

- Join ConventionOfStates.com

Article 5 is the proper way to _evolve_ [22] the Constitution.

A democracy runs on _____[23]; a republic runs on _____[24]. The Amendment process is designed to be slow to keep passion out of it.

The Founding Fathers designed the amendment process so that if an amendment passes, it is because _____ _____[25] themselves supported it.

Article ____[26] gives two options for how to amend the Constitution.

Option 1: Congressional Proposals

When _____[27] of both the House and Senate adopt proposed Amendments, they are sent to the states for ratification and _____[28] of the states must ratify for the Amendment to become part of the Constitution.

Option 2: State Proposals

When _____[29] of states apply, Congress must call a convention of the states for proposing amendments. Any amendments proposed at the convention must still be ratified by _____[30] of the states before the Amendment would become part of the Constitution.

All it takes to kill a Constitutional amendment is one legislative body from each of only _____[31] states.

It does not _____[32] the Constitution to use the Constitution.

A convention of states is a way for the states to _____ _____[33] against encroachment from the Federal government.

Visit ConventionOfStates.com for more information & to see the simulated convention filmed at Colonial Williamsburg.

Article V limits the changes made to "_____
_____[34]," thus preventing the creation of a whole new Constitution.

The states can _____[35] their delegates to the Convention of States if the delegates do not honor the wishes of their respective states.

Finally ye . . . whose power it is to save or destroy your country, consider well the important trust . . . which God... has put into your hands. To God and posterity, you are accountable for them. . . Let not your children have reason to curse you for giving up those rights, and prostrating those institutions which your fathers delivered to you.[xxxiv]

- Reverend Matthias Burnett

DUTY IS OURS, RESULTS ARE GOD'S.
- John Quincy Adams

BECOME A BIBLICAL CITIZENSHIP COACH AND REPLICATE THIS CLASS OVER AND OVER AGAIN!

SIGN UP TODAY AT BiblicalCitizens.com

APPENDIX A:

CONSTITUTION AT A GLANCE

APPENDIX A:
U.S. CONSTITUTION AT A GLANCE

ARTICLES:

I	=	Congress
II	=	Presidency
III	=	Courts
IV	=	States; Republic
V	=	Amendment Process
VI	=	Debts, Supremacy, oath, no religious test
VII	=	Ratification & Attestation

AMENDMENTS:

1 -10	=	Bill of Rights (see below)
12, 20, 22, 23, 25	=	Presidency
11	=	Judiciary (suits against states)
17, 20, 27	=	Congress (Sen elections, terms, $$$)
13, 14, 15	=	End slavery & establish Civil Rights
15, 19, 24, 26	=	Voting Rights (race, gender, $$$, age)
16	=	Income Tax
18 & 21	=	To drink or not to drink

BILL OF RIGHTS:

1st	=	religion; speech; press; assembly; petition
2nd	=	individual right to bear arms
3rd	=	quartering of soldiers
4th	=	searches & seizures
5th	=	Grand Jury; Double Jeopardy; Self-Incrimination; Due Process; private property takings clause
6th	=	speedy public jury trial; witnesses; attorney
7th	=	civil jury trial
8th	=	excessive fines & bail; cruel & unusual
9th	=	individual rights not enumerated or limited
10th	=	fed pwr limited/enumerated; rest left to states/people

APPENDIX B:

WHAT ABOUT SEPARATION OF CHURCH AND STATE?

(excerpted from Chapter 7 of *Freedom's Frame* by Rick Green)

APPENDIX B:

WHAT ABOUT SEPARATION OF CHURCH AND STATE?

(excerpted from Chapter 7 of *Freedom's Frame* by Rick Green)

Almighty God, we acknowledge our dependence upon Thee, and we beg Thy blessings upon us, our parents, our teachers, and our Country. [xxxv]

These are the simple words of a voluntary prayer, which the Supreme Court ruled as being unconstitutional in 1962 and banned it from being recited by children in our public schools. The court based their actions entirely upon one phrase, *"separation of church and state."*

Wherever I speak on college campuses, almost every student in the audience is familiar with that phrase. The words, "separation of church and state" have become the political mantra of this generation. However, those same students are seldom as familiar with quotes taken from the Declaration of Independence or the Constitution, and when I ask them to tell me in which document the phrase "separation of church and state" is found, invariably someone will respond, "It is in the Declaration of Independence."

When I answer, "No, you will not find it in the Declaration," someone else will respond, "It is in the Constitution."

An answer of, "No, it is not in the Constitution either," often sparks a heated debate (especially at law schools) with a chorus of objectors clamoring to remind me of the Constitutional Separation of Church and State found in the First Amendment.

To which I reply, "Are you sure it is found in the First Amendment? Let's look and see…"

> *Congress shall make no law respecting an establishment*
> *of religion, or prohibiting the free exercise thereof. . .*
> *lxxxvi*

…anyone see the word "separation?" How about the words "church" or "state?"

Of course, someone will then say, "Well, that is not what it says, but that is what it means." Already convinced they can determine the intent of the statute, we begin a discussion on legislative intent.

The Meaning of "is"

To understand the "intent" of the legislators who pass any law, one must look at the journal that recorded the discussions that took place at the time the law was being debated. Or one must read the writings of the legislators who passed the law. Doing so is akin to cracking open their heads and peering into their minds to find out what they were thinking and, therefore, what they were intending.

The system still works the same way today as it did in the beginning. A legislator will address the floor from the front of the room and explain the bill, stating the case for why it should become law. The debate then begins. Opponents will ask questions or challenge sections of the bill. Supporters will throw "softball questions" at the author to help bring out the full meaning of the bill. All of this discussion is then transcribed and included in the journal, which can then be read by any interested person.

Why do they do this? Because, if years after a law is passed, confusion arises about certain portions of its meaning, or questions are raised of its intent, the answers can be found in the Annals. Let's face it, sometimes the legal language that is found in pieces of legislation can be hard to decipher, even for our elected officials who have been trained in understanding these documents. At times, even Presidents can have difficulty with grasping the true meaning of the simplest of language, (such as the meaning of the word "is") and they may need some help in coming to a fuller comprehension of the intent and meaning of the law.

The journal allows us to go back and discover what the legislators were thinking on the day they were discussing the law. What did they envision as the intended and expected application? This information was deemed so necessary to our correct interpretation of intent that a provision in the Constitution requires that everything said on the floor of the House and Senate be recorded in a journal, for this very purpose.[xxxvii]

This means that we can go all the way back to the discussions held between our Founding Fathers and discover exactly what those Congressmen intended when they passed the laws that govern us today. All we need to do is simply open up the Annals of Congress.

If we go back and read those transcripts, we will find that considerable time was spent debating the First Amendment to the Constitution. From June 8th to September 25th 1789, Congress discussed the details and parameters of this amendment. Yet nowhere in the Annals of Congress or the writings of the Founding Fathers who drafted the First Amendment, will you find the phrase "separation of church and state."

Original Intent of the First Amendment

Fisher Ames provided the wording for the First Amendment in the House of Representatives. He did not say anything about "separation of church and state" in his debate, nor may it be inferred as his intent. In fact, Fisher Ames said something that would be ruled unconstitutional because of the court's modern application of that very phrase, "separation of church and state." He said, *"Not only should the Bible be in our schools, it should be the primary textbook of our schools."*[xxxviii]

Earlier, at the time of the Constitutional Convention, the founders discussed the individual rights of American citizens, which would later become the Bill of Rights. How many times did they mention the phrase "separation of church and state?" Zero. They did not talk about it once.

The phrase "separation of church and state" was not even introduced into the American vernacular until a little over a decade after the First Amendment was adopted. The phrase is exactly that - a phrase. It is not a statute, it is not a law, and it is not an amendment to the Constitution. It is simply a phrase lifted from a letter written by one of our Founding Fathers, Thomas Jefferson.

Jefferson was writing to the Danbury Baptist Association on January 1, 1802, in response to a letter wherein they raised their concerns about religious liberty ever being infringed by the American government. Jefferson responded that this would not occur because the Constitution builds "a wall of separation between Church and State."[xxxix] So much has been erroneously inferred from that one statement. (I encourage you to read David Barton's article in the November 2003 issue of the Notre Dame Law Review for a more thorough treatment of Jefferson's intent.)

Simply stated, Jefferson was using the phrase to describe the Free Exercise Clause of the First Amendment, which says, *"or prohibiting the free exercise thereof."* The protection of our rights to live out our faith without government interference is what was being expressed both in the letter and in the First Amendment.

The Supreme Court twisted the meaning of the First Amendment by isolating those eight words from this personal letter from Jefferson.[xl] They did not even consider the letter in its full context.[xli] Then, in 1962, the Court used the phrase to completely remove God from all governmental institutions.[xlii] It is amazing how the court can ignore history and rewrite it to fulfill their particular agenda and purpose.

We've Got the Wrong Guy

Perhaps even worse than misapplying Jefferson's words is the fact that Jefferson's words were used in the first place as a means for discovering the intent of the First Amendment. Actually, Thomas Jefferson and his words "separation of church and state" are irrelevant when it comes to interpreting the intended meaning of the First Amendment because Jefferson did not give us the Constitution or the Bill of Rights.

When a biographer wrote to Thomas Jefferson, to congratulate him for his influence on the Constitution, his response was,

> *One passage of the paper you enclosed must be corrected. It is the following. 'I will say it was yourself more than any other individual that planned and established the Constitution.'*[xliii]

Jefferson pointed out to the biographer that he *"was in Europe when the Constitution was planned, and never saw it until after it had been established.'*[xliv]

Nor was Thomas Jefferson one of the Congressmen that passed the Bill of Rights, which contains the First Amendment.

So, arguing what the framers' intent was by using Thomas Jefferson as an expert witness on the First Amendment is the same as having a murder trial where the judge allows those who were not at the scene of the murder to come forth and tell us what happened. It is intellectually dishonest and a piece of cleverly crafted creative history at best, to say that Thomas Jefferson's words provide the intent for the First Amendment. To understand the original intent of the First Amendment, you must scrutinize the thoughts of those who took part in the debate, the ones who actually gave us the First Amendment.

That debate emphasized the need to avoid another Church of England being established in America. In other words, they were trying to prevent a national denomination from being forced upon the citizens. None of their comments reflected intent to separate religious principles from government or from the public square. Just the opposite: they wanted to foster free expression, not political oppression.

For those who still want to rely on Jefferson as their expert regarding the First Amendment, it should not go unnoticed that exactly two days after writing his letter to the Danbury Baptists, he attended the weekly church service being held at the U.S. Capitol. These were religious services that he had helped to start and faithfully attended throughout the remainder of his presidency.[xlv]

It appears that Jefferson's views were far removed from the interpretation of them by our modern courts today. Would Jefferson, a man who himself established and attended religious services on federal property while holding the office of the President, really think that it was against the good of our nation or our citizens for children to pray for their teachers, parents, and country at the beginning of each school day? You decide.

Appendix C:

The Declaration of Independence

Appendix C:
The Declaration of Independence

IN CONGRESS, July 4, 1776.

The unanimous Declaration of the thirteen united States of America,

When in the Course of human events, it becomes necessary for one people to dissolve the political bands which have connected them with another, and to assume among the powers of the earth, the separate and equal station to which the Laws of Nature and of Nature's God entitle them, a decent respect to the opinions of mankind requires that they should declare the causes which impel them to the separation.

We hold these truths to be self-evident, that all men are created equal, that they are endowed by their Creator with certain unalienable Rights, that among these are Life, Liberty and the pursuit of Happiness. --That to secure these rights, Governments are instituted among Men, deriving their just powers from the consent of the governed, -- That whenever any Form of Government becomes destructive of these ends, it is the Right of the People to alter or to abolish it, and to institute new Government, laying its foundation on such principles and organizing its powers in such form, as to them shall seem most likely to effect their Safety and Happiness. Prudence, indeed, will dictate that Governments long established should not be changed for light and transient causes; and accordingly all experience hath shewn, that mankind are more disposed to suffer, while evils are sufferable, than to right themselves by abolishing the forms to which they are accustomed. But when a long train of abuses and usurpations, pursuing invariably the same Object evinces a design to reduce them under absolute Despotism, it is their right, it is their duty, to throw off such Government, and to provide new Guards for their future security.--Such has been the patient sufferance of these Colonies; and such is now the necessity which constrains them to alter their former Systems of Government. The history of the present King of Great Britain is a history of repeated injuries and usurpations, all having in direct object the establishment of an absolute Tyranny over these States. To prove this, let Facts be submitted to a candid world.

He has refused his Assent to Laws, the most wholesome and necessary for the public good.

He has forbidden his Governors to pass Laws of immediate and pressing importance, unless suspended in their operation till his Assent should be obtained; and when so suspended, he has utterly neglected to attend to them.

He has refused to pass other Laws for the accommodation of large districts of people, unless those people would relinquish the right of Representation in the Legislature, a right inestimable to them and formidable to tyrants only.

He has called together legislative bodies at places unusual, uncomfortable, and distant from the depository of their public Records, for the sole purpose of fatiguing them into compliance with his measures.

He has dissolved Representative Houses repeatedly, for opposing with manly firmness his invasions on the rights of the people.

He has refused for a long time, after such dissolutions, to cause others to be elected; whereby the Legislative powers, incapable of Annihilation, have returned to the People at large for their exercise; the State remaining in the mean time exposed to all the dangers of invasion from without, and convulsions within.

He has endeavoured to prevent the population of these States; for that purpose obstructing the Laws for Naturalization of Foreigners; refusing to pass others to encourage their migrations hither, and raising the conditions of new Appropriations of Lands.

He has obstructed the Administration of Justice, by refusing his Assent to Laws for establishing Judiciary powers.

He has made Judges dependent on his Will alone, for the tenure of their offices, and the amount and payment of their salaries.

He has erected a multitude of New Offices, and sent hither swarms of Officers to harrass our people, and eat out their substance.

He has kept among us, in times of peace, Standing Armies without the Consent of our legislatures.

He has affected to render the Military independent of and superior to the Civil power.

He has combined with others to subject us to a jurisdiction foreign to our constitution, and unacknowledged by our laws; giving his Assent to their Acts of pretended Legislation:

For Quartering large bodies of armed troops among us:

For protecting them, by a mock Trial, from punishment for any Murders which they should commit on the Inhabitants of these States:

For cutting off our Trade with all parts of the world:

For imposing Taxes on us without our Consent:

For depriving us in many cases, of the benefits of Trial by Jury:

For transporting us beyond Seas to be tried for pretended offences

For abolishing the free System of English Laws in a neighbouring Province, establishing therein an Arbitrary government, and enlarging its Boundaries so as to render it at once an example and fit instrument for introducing the same absolute rule into these Colonies:

For taking away our Charters, abolishing our most valuable Laws, and altering fundamentally the Forms of our Governments:

For suspending our own Legislatures, and declaring themselves invested with power to legislate for us in all cases whatsoever.

He has abdicated Government here, by declaring us out of his Protection and waging War against us.

He has plundered our seas, ravaged our Coasts, burnt our towns, and destroyed the lives of our people.

He is at this time transporting large Armies of foreign Mercenaries to compleat the works of death, desolation and tyranny, already begun with circumstances of Cruelty & perfidy scarcely paralleled in the most barbarous ages, and totally unworthy the Head of a civilized nation.

He has constrained our fellow Citizens taken Captive on the high Seas to bear Arms against their Country, to become the executioners of their friends and Brethren, or to fall themselves by their Hands.

He has excited domestic insurrections amongst us, and has endeavoured to bring on the inhabitants of our frontiers, the merciless Indian Savages, whose known rule of warfare, is an undistinguished destruction of all ages, sexes and conditions.

In every stage of these Oppressions We have Petitioned for Redress in the most humble terms: Our repeated Petitions have been answered only by repeated injury. A Prince whose character is thus marked by every act which may define a Tyrant, is unfit to be the ruler of a free people.

Nor have We been wanting in attentions to our Brittish brethren. We have warned them from time to time of attempts by their legislature to extend an unwarrantable jurisdiction over us. We have reminded them of the circumstances of our emigration and settlement here. We have appealed to their native justice and magnanimity, and we have conjured them by the ties of our common kindred to disavow these usurpations, which, would inevitably interrupt our connections and correspondence. They too have been deaf to the voice of justice and of consanguinity. We must, therefore, acquiesce in the necessity, which denounces our Separation, and hold them, as we hold the rest of mankind, Enemies in War, in Peace Friends.

We, therefore, the Representatives of the united States of America, in General Congress, Assembled, appealing to the Supreme Judge of the world for the rectitude of our intentions, do, in the Name, and by Authority of the good People of these Colonies, solemnly publish and declare, That these United Colonies are, and of Right ought to be Free and Independent States; that they are Absolved from all Allegiance to the British Crown, and that all political connection between them and the State of Great Britain, is and ought to be totally dissolved; and that as Free and Independent States, they have full Power to levy War, conclude Peace, contract Alliances, establish Commerce, and to do all other Acts and Things which Independent States may of right do. And for the support of this Declaration, with a firm reliance on the protection of divine Providence, we mutually pledge to each other our Lives, our Fortunes and our sacred Honor.

The 56 signatures on the Declaration:

Connecticut:
Roger Sherman
Samuel Huntington
William Williams
Oliver Wolcott

Delaware:
Caesar Rodney
George Read
Thomas McKean

Georgia:
Button Gwinnett
Lyman Hall
George Walton

Maryland:
Samuel Chase
William Paca
Thomas Stone
Charles Carroll of
    Carrollton

Massachusetts:
Samuel Adams
John Adams
John Hancock
Robert Treat Paine
Elbridge Gerry

New Hampshire:
Josiah Bartlett
William Whipple
Matthew Thornton

New Jersey:
Richard Stockton
John Witherspoon
Francis Hopkinson
John Hart
Abraham Clark

New York:
William Floyd
Philip Livingston
Francis Lewis
Lewis Morris

North Carolina:
William Hooper
Joseph Hewes
John Penn

South Carolina:
Edward Rutledge
Thomas Heyward, Jr.
Thomas Lynch, Jr.
Arthur Middleton

Pennsylvania:
Robert Morris
Benjamin Rush
Benjamin Franklin
John Morton
George Clymer
James Smith
George Taylor
James Wilson
George Ross

Rhode Island:
Stephen Hopkins
William Ellery

Virginia:
George Wythe
Richard Henry Lee
Thomas Jefferson
Benjamin Harrison
Thomas Nelson, Jr.
Francis Lightfoot Lee
Carter Braxton

APPENDIX D:

ENDNOTES & ANSWER KEY

APPENDIX D:
ENDNOTES & ANSWER KEY

i   John M. Taylor, *Garfield of Ohio: The Available Man* (New York: W. W. Norton and Company, Inc.), p. 180. Quoted from "A Century of Progress," by James A. Garfield, published in Atlantic, July 1877.[i]

ii   Donald S. Lutz, *The Origins of American Constitutionalism* (Baton Rouge, LA: Louisiana State University Press, 1988), p. 143.

iii   John Jay, The *Correspondence and Public Papers of John Jay*, Henry P. Johnston, editor (New York: G. P. Putnam's Sons, 1890), Vol. I, pp. 163–164, from his "Charge to the Grand Jury of Ulster County" on September 9, 1777.

iv   Abraham Lincoln, Draft of the Gettysburg Address: Nicolay Copy, November 1863; Series 3, General Correspondence, 1837-1897; The Abraham Lincoln Papers at the Library of Congress, Manuscript Division (Washington, D. C.: American Memory Project, [2000-02])

v   Thomas Jefferson, *Memoir, Correspondence, and Miscellanies, From the Papers of Thomas Jefferson*, Thomas Jefferson Randolph, editor (Boston: Gray and Bowen, 1830), Vol. IV, p. 373, to Judge William Johnson on June 12, 1823.

vi   Joseph Story, *Commentaries on the Constitution of the United States* (Boston: Hilliard, Gray, and Company, 1833), Vol. I, p. 383, § 400.

vii   John Quincy Adams, The Jubilee of the Constitution (New York: Samuel Colman, 1839), p. 54.

viii Samuel Adams, The Writing of Samuel Adams, at 357 of Volume IV (Collected & edited by Harry Alonzo Cushing, G.P. Putnam's Sons 1908).

ix   Gulf, c. & s. F. R. Co. V. Ellis, 165 U.S. 150 (1897)

x   The Declaration of Independence, para. 2 (U.S. 1776).

xi   *George Washington, Address of George Washington, President of the United States ... Preparatory to His Declination* 22–23 (Baltimore: George and Henry S. Keatinge, 1796).[xi]

xii   Thomas Jefferson, *Notes on the State of Virginia* (Philadelphia: Matthew Carey, 1794), Query XVIII, p. 237.[xii]

xiii James Madison, *Notes of Debates in the Federal Convention of 1787*, at 209-10 (reprinted NY: W.W. Norton & Co., 1987) (1787).

xiv   Alexander Hamilton, John Jay, & James Madison, *The Federalist* (Philadelphia: Benjamin Warner, 1818), p. 194, James Madison, Federalist #38; see also Federalist #2 (p. 12) and Federalist #20 (p. 105) for other acknowledgments of the blessings of Providence upon America.

xv   Hamilton, Alexander. 1787. Christine F. Hart, *One Nation Under God* (NJ: American Tract Society, reprinted by Gospel Tract Society, Inc.), p. 2. D.P. Diffine, Ph.D., *One Nation Under God—How Close a Separation?* (Searcy, Arkansas: Harding University, Belden Center for Private Enterprise Education, 6th edition, 1992), p. 9.

xvi   Letters To The Marquis De Lafayette, February 7 & May28, 1788.

xvii   Thomas Jefferson, *The Jeffersonian Cyclopedia* (Funk & Wagnalls company, 1900), page 326

xviii   Bradford's History of Plymouth Plantation, 1606-1646. Ed. William T. Davis. New York: Charles Scribner's Sons, 1908

xix   Ibid

xx   Madison's Notes to the Debates in the Federal Convention of 1787, 14 August 1787. John Francis Mercer was a Maryland Delegate to the Convention.

xxi   "Supreme Court Justice Clarence Thomas' Wriston Lecture to the Manhattan Institute," The Wall Street Journal, 20 October 2008, p. A19

xxii   James Madison letter to Andrew Stevenson; 27 Nov. 1830

xxiii   John Adams, *Works,* Vol. VI, p. 484, to John Taylor on April 15, 1814.

xxiv   Benjamin Rush, *The Letters of Benjamin Rush,* L. H. Butterfield, editor (Princeton: Princeton University Press for the American Philosophical Society, 1951), Vol. I, p. 523, to John Adams on July 21, 1789.

xxv   Ex Parte Mccardle, 74 U.S. 506 (Wall.) (1868)

xxvi   U.S. Const. Amend. I.

xxvii   U.S. Const. Art. I, § 5, cl. 3.

xxviii   William Parker Cutler and Julia Perkins Cutler, *Life, Journal, and Correspondence of Rev. Manasseh Cutler* (Cincinnati: Colin Robert Clarke & Co., 1888), Vol. II, p. 66, 119, letter to Joseph Torrey, January 4, 1802. Cutler meant that Jefferson attended church on January 3, 1802, for the first time as President. Bishop Claggett's letter of February 18, 1801, already revealed that as Vice-President, Jefferson went to church services in the House.

xxix   Jared Sparks, *The Life of Governeur Morris* (Boston: Gray and Bowen, 1832), Vol. III, p. 483, from his "Notes on the Form of a Constitution for France."

xxx   Constitutions (1813), p. 364, "An Ordinance of the Territory of the United States Northwest of the River Ohio," Article III.

xxxi   James Wilson, *The Works of the Honourable James Wilson,* Bird Wilson, editor (Philadelphia: Bronson and Chauncey, 1804), Vol. I, pp. 104–106, "Of the General Principles of Law and Obligation."

xxxii   John Adams, "On Private Revenge," *Boston Gazette,* September 5, 1763.

xxxiii   Noah Webster, *The History of the United States* (New Haven: Durrie and Peck, 1832), pp. 336–337, ¶49.

xxxiv   Matthias Burnett, *An Election Sermon, Preached at Hartford, on the Day of the Anniversary Election,* May 12, 1803, at 26-27 (Hartford: Hudson & Goodwin, 1803).

xxxv   *Engel v. Vitale,* 370 U.S. 421, 422 (1962).

xxxvi   U.S. Const. Amend. I.

xxxvii   U.S. Const. Art. I, § 5, cl. 3.

xxxviii Compiled By Friends, *Works of Fisher Ames* 134 (Boston: T. B. Wait & Co., 1809).

xxxix   Letter to the Danbury Baptist Association (January 1, 1802), *in* Thomas Jefferson, Jefferson Writings 510 (Merril D. Peterson et al. eds., 1984) (1781).

xl   Everson v. Board of Education, 330 U.S. 1 (1947).

[xli] Thomas Jefferson, Letter to the Danbury Baptist Association, *in Thomas Jefferson, Jefferson Writings* 510 (Merrill D. Peterson et al. eds., 1984) (1802): *Believing with you that religion is a matter which lies solely between man and his God, that he owes account to none other for faith or his worship, that the legislative powers of government reach actions only, and not opinions, I contemplate with solemn reverence that act of the whole American people which declared that their legislature should "make no law respecting an establishment of religion, or prohibiting the free exercise thereof," thus building a wall of separation between Church and State.*

[xlii] *Engle* v. *Vitale*, 370 U.S. 421 (1962).

[xliii] Letter to Dr. Joseph Priestly (Washington ed., 441). <http://etext.lib.virginia.edu/etcbin/foley-page?id=JCE1686>.

[xliv] *Id.*

[xlv] William Parker Cutler and Julia Perkins Cutler, *Life, Journal, and Correspondence of Rev. Manasseh Cutler* (Cincinnati: Colin Robert Clarke & Co., 1888), Vol. II, p. 66, 119, letter to Joseph Torrey, January 4, 1802. Cutler meant that Jefferson attended church on January 3, 1802, for the first time as President. Bishop Claggett's letter of February 18, 1801, already revealed that as Vice-President, Jefferson went to church services in the House.

ANSWER KEY

Week One

1. disciples
2. nations
3. everything
4. God's Word
5. We the People
6. frequent recurrence
7. ourselves
8. one true God
9. Morality, Education, Law, & Liberty
10. heart
11. good laws
12. God's laws
13. justice and mercy
14. full armor
15. liberty
16. faith, morality, laws
17. you and me
18. restore

Week Two

1. seed-plot
2. self-government
3. family, government, church
4. Biblical citizens
5. tend His garden
6. Business, Government, Family, Religion, Media, Education, Entertainment
7. 17
8. Locke
9. Blackstone
10. Montesquieu

Week Two (continued)

[11] The Bible

[12] castle

[13] commanding officer

[14] James Otis

[15] writs of assistance

[16] house

[17] castle

[18] God-given

[19] papers

[20] warrants

[21] cause

[22] place

[23] persons

[24] things

[25] Jamestown and Plymouth

[26] 1620

[27] 20

[28] elected

[29] American Revolution

[30] Favoured

[31] black

[32] slave trade

[33] first

[34] slavery

[35] 40

Week Three

[1] truth

[2] Christians

[3] religion

[4] socialism

[5] opinion

Week Three (continued)

6   America

7   lie

8   truth

9   God's Word

10   Bible

11   find

12   courage

13   love

14   find

15   defend

16   knowing, perceive, defend, assert

17   formula

18   defend

19   assert

20   principles

21   moral and religious

22   God, country, families

23   great enemy

24   August 2, 1776

25   death warrant

26   Nathan Hale

27   earn

28   increased devotion

29   YOU (write YOUR name in this blank!)

30   Celebrate Freedom Week

31   quick start guide

32   identify, protect, preserve

33   original intent

34   amended

35   original text

36   original intent

37   principle

Week Three (continued)

[38] everyone

[39] platform

[40] smart

Week Four

[1] articles of incorporation

[2] by-laws

[3] Self-evident Truths

[4] Endowed by Our Creator

[5] Consent of the Governed

[6] The Pursuit of Happiness

[7] liberty WITH God

[8] liberty withOUT God

[9] God to the King to the people

[10] God to the people to government

[11] give

[12] take

[13] basis of liberty

[14] Benjamin

[15] confusion and discontent

[16] private property & free enterprise

[17] wise decisions

[18] Creator

[19] limited government

[20] government

[21] Inalienable rights

[22] rights

[23] authority

[24] protect

[25] provide

[26] prosperous

[27] fixed moral

Week Four (continued)

28 anarchy

29 consent

30 rights

31 moral law

32 change their government

33 from the people

34 copied

35 1,500

36 preached

37 pulpit

38 John Wise

39 legally binding

40 4

41 2

42 8

43 1

44 Sec 8, Cl 12

45 Art 1, Sec 8, Cl 14

46 3rd Amendment

47 6th & 7th Amendments

48 individual welfare

49 God

50 22nd

51 Franklin Delano Roosevelt

52 state

53 state

54 vote for president

55 Congress

56 President

57 Courts

58 States; Republic

59 Amendment Process

Week Four (continued)

60 Debts, Supremacy, oath, no religious test
61 Ratification & Attestation
62 Bill of Rights
63 President (EC, dates, 2 terms, DC, incapacitation)
64 Judiciary (suits against states)
65 Congress (Sen elections, terms, pay raises)
66 End slavery & establish civil rights
67 Voting Rights (race, gender, $$$, age)
68 Income Tax
69 To drink or not to drink!
70 religion; speech; press; assembly; petition
71 right to bear arms
72 quartering of soldiers
73 searches & seizures
74 grand jury; double jeopardy; self-incrimination; due process; private property takings
75 speedy public jury trial; witnesses; attorney
76 civil jury trial & common law
77 excessive fines & bail; cruel & unusual punishment
78 individual rights NOT enumerated
79 federal powers ltd/enumerated; rest left to states/people
80 17th
81 U.S. Senators
82 applies
83 minority
84 participate
85 18th

Week Five

1 limited government
2 moral law
3 jurisdictional

Week Five (continued)

4   promote and support
5   big to fail
6   federal government
7   federal government
8   states
9   to itself
10   debts
11   defense
12   welfare
13   theft
14   general
15   local
16   one
17   regular
18   foreign
19   states
20   Indian tribes
21   micro-manage
22   individual enterprise
23   distrust of power
24   levels of government
25   spirit
26   ample reward
27   3%-6%
28   bottom up

Week Six

1   election day sermon
2   faithfully executed
3   laws
4   men
5   themselves aside

Week Six (continued)

[6] president

[7] people

[8] states

[9] popular vote

[10] sufficient vote

[11] distribution

[12] big cities

[13] pure democracy

[14] three

[15] four

[16] in the movies

[17] Ronald Reagan

[18] George W. Bush (43)

[19] Washington

[20] Congress

[21] passed

[22] afraid of God

[23] rewards and punishments

[24] evolution

[25] all law

[26] 4

[27] lifetime

[28] as it existed

[29] as they want it to be

[30] taken control

[31] lack of accountability

[32] lifetime appointments

[33] Alexander Hamilton, John Jay, & James Madison

[34] Legislative

[35] closest to the people

[36] Judiciary

[37] two branches

Week Six (continued)

38 responsibility

39 Congress

40 agenda

41 good behavior

42 try

43 contradicting

44 rudeness

45 high-handedness

46 bridle

Week Seven

1 inalienable rights

2 take away

3 protect inalienable rights

4 one step

5 religion; speech; press; assembly; petition

6 nowhere

7 journal

8 One, Five

9 none

10 Thomas Jefferson

11 infringe

12 single national denomination

13 the U.S. Capitol

14 kneeling in prayer

15 "Forbid it, Almighty God!"

16 Abraham Baldwin

17 chaplain

18 American Bible Society

19 William Samuel Johnson

20 Maryland Bible Society

21 Gouverneur Morris

Week Seven (continued)

[22] religion, morality

[23] James Wilson

[24] worship

[25] religion

[26] property

[27] 1640

[28] Blackstone's Commentaries on the Law

[29] revealed Himself

[30] Scriptures

[31] violating

[32] protect

[33] end slavery

[34] boundaries

[35] public use

[36] public purpose

Week Eight

[1] September 17th

[2] 90%

[3] ambassador

[4] incrementalism

[5] Vote

[6] chosen

[7] 20

[8] 36

[9] 537

[10] leaders

[11] principles

[12] candidates

[13] actions

[14] politician

[15] patriot

Week Eight (continued)

16 Senators

17 state

18 support

19 republic

20 amendment

21 live

22 amend

23 passion

24 reason

25 the people

26 Five

27 two-thirds (34 total)

28 three-fourths (38 total)

29 two-thirds (34 total)

30 three-fourths (38)

31 13

32 endanger

33 push back

34 this Constitution

35 recall

APPENDIX E:
THE CONSTITUTION MADE EASY
By Michael Holler

**The following is included with the
permission of Michael Holler**

The CONSTITUTION MADE *Easy*

THE UNITED STATES CONSTITUTION

Compared Side by Side with

THE UNITED STATES CONSTITUTION

In Modern English

ISBN 978-1-60725-330-3

Published in the United States by
The Friends of Freedom, Inc.
PO Box 7333, Woodland Park, CO 80863

Manufactured in the United States of America

GUIDE TO UNDERSTANDING
AND ENJOYING
THE CONSTITUTION MADE EASY

For most people, reading the *United States Constitution* is difficult, and no wonder! It was written in "legalese," and most of it is more than 200 years old. But now *The Constitution Made Easy* not only offers a modernized version for easier reading; it actually makes the meaning of the original seem to jump off the page!

Great effort was made to preserve the original meaning and intent of the Founding Fathers in this modern English version; but by keeping the original side-by-side for comparison, *The Constitution Made Easy* becomes a reference you can trust. The *Constitution* and all of the *Amendments* in this volume were carefully copied from the version maintained by the United States Government at the National Archives. The reader is invited to visit the Archives at: www.archives.gov/exhibits.

Here are a few facts and some unique features of *The Constitution Made Easy* that will make your reading more enjoyable, and avoid unnecessary confusion.

The original Constitution will *always* be on the left-hand page, and the modern English version will *always* be on the right. The two versions look very different from each other, and the headers at the top of the page confirm which version is below it.

Now, here are a few facts about the *original*. The body of the Constitution has seven large divisions called *Articles*. Each Article discusses a new subject, such as Congress, the President or the Supreme Court. The divisions within Articles are called *Sections*, and the divisions within Sections are called *Clauses*. Any given *Clause* is normally referred to by its location, such as Article I, Section VIII, Clause VII. (This particular *Clause* concerns the Post Office.) Roman numerals are used in the original.

A modern numbering plan was adopted in the modern version, so that same Clause would be referred to as Article 1, Section 8, Clause 7. A *shorthand* way of referring to it would be simply **1.8.7** (one-dot-eight-dot-seven). At the end of the Articles are the signatures of the State delegates. When the Constitution was first approved (ratified) this is all there was.

Then there are 27 *Amendments* that come after these first seven Articles. An Amendment is sometimes referred to as an *Article of Amendment.* So like other *Articles*, it may be divided into *Sections*, and several of them have been. In the modern version, one of these *Sections* (Amendment 20, Section 3) has even been divided into two *Clauses*.

Until now, one of the great barriers to understanding the Constitution was that an Amendment sometimes modified just a few words, and sometimes it completely replaced (or *superceded*) one or more full Clauses. In the National Archives version, the language that has been replaced or modified is underlined, and then the Amendment that affected it is [cited in brackets like this].

Without a modern version, readers may find themselves jumping forward to find the Amendment, then jumping back to the original, and trying to mentally *integrate* the effects of the changes. In some cases, this can be so frustrating that even a good reader may decide to put the Constitution down "for now anyway" (and sometimes does not return to it).

Now, *The Constitution Made Easy* does this work for you. All of the effects of the Amendments are included *right in the text*. If the effect was modest, only the affected words or phrases will be added or replaced. If the effect was substantial (as you will see in Article 2, Section 1), then whole Amendments may be included in the modern version to bring the content current. These Amendments are often much longer than the language they replace.

In these instances there will be more Clauses in the modern version than in the original, and so the numbering will be different. This also creates "gaps," or blank lines, in a few places in the original. To keep it clear, the original will have [bracketed information] referring to the Amendment that replaced the original wording, and the modern version will likewise refer to it, [either in brackets] or a footnote. There should never be any real need to flash back and forth between the original and the Amendments in order to understand the current meaning.

The Constitution Made Easy

It is easy to tell where paragraphs in the original begin and end, even if there is "white space" in the middle. If any line is indented, this indicates a new paragraph in the original. If it begins at the left margin, it is a continuation of the paragraph above it.

The full texts of all of the Amendments are still included after the "amended" body of the Constitution, so some of the language will be seen for a second time. This will be especially noticeable in the 12th, 20th and 25th Amendments which greatly affected Article 2, Section 1. Also noteworthy is Amendment 17 which affected the election of Senators (Article 1, Section 3).

One more note about the *shorthand* numbering plan. To make it more apparent whether the numbers refer to the body of the Constitution, or to an Amendment, the letter "C" is added in front of the numbers to indicate the body of the Constitution, and the letter "A" is added in front to indicate an Amendment. So for example, **C:1.8.7** indicates the Constitution: Article 1, Section 8, Clause 7; while Amendment 20, Section 3, Clause 2 would be written **A:20.3.2**. These are usually in **bold type** (as shown), for ease of reference.

As a final thought, the *Constitution Made Easy* is much easier to understand than the original, but is not intended to replace it for serious study. Almost anyone can read this modern version (the odd-numbered pages) in under 30 minutes, and should be able to grasp the essential propositions and themes. It is hoped that this will then inspire the reader to read and study the original, perhaps using the modern version and footnotes as tools.

The Constitution is "the supreme law of the land." Virtually every elected and public official in America takes an oath to uphold it. The President promises to "preserve, protect and defend" it. The organization chart of the United States Government shows Congress, the President and the Supreme Court *underneath* the Constitution.

The Constitution has been called the greatest governing document ever written by man. Understanding it is worth the effort, and now easier than ever before. Enjoy!

The Constitution of the United States

We the People of the United States, in Order to form a more perfect Union, establish Justice, insure domestic Tranquility, provide for the common defence, promote the general Welfare, and secure the Blessings of Liberty to ourselves and our Posterity, do ordain and establish this Constitution for the United States of America.

Article. I.

Section. 1.

All legislative Powers herein granted shall be vested in a Congress of the United States, which shall consist of a Senate and House of Representatives.

Section. 2.

The House of Representatives shall be composed of Members chosen every second Year by the People of the several States, and the Electors in each State shall have the Qualifications requisite for Electors of the most numerous Branch of the State Legislature.

No Person shall be a Representative who shall not have attained to the Age of twenty five Years, and been seven Years a Citizen of the United States, and who shall not, when elected, be an Inhabitant of that State in which he shall be chosen.

Representatives and direct Taxes shall be apportioned among the several States which may be included within this Union, according to their respective Numbers, which shall be determined by adding to the whole Number of free Persons, including those bound to Service for a Term of Years, and excluding Indians not taxed, three fifths of all other Persons. [Changed by Section 2 of the 14th Amendment, and the 16th Amendment]

The Constitution Made Easy

The Constitution of the United States

We the people of the United States have created and agreed to this Constitution for the United States of America. We have done this in order to make our Union stronger, set standards for justice, keep the peace at home, provide for our common defense, promote our general well-being, and make sure that the blessings of liberty continue for ourselves and our descendents.

Article 1

Section 1

All of the law-making Powers granted by this agreement will be entrusted to a Congress of the United States. Congress will consist of a Senate and a House of Representatives.

Section 2

1.2.1   The members of the House of Representatives will be elected every two years by the people in each of the States. Each State has a standard it uses to decide who is allowed to vote[1] for its own State legislature.[2] This same standard must be used to determine who is allowed to vote for members of the House of Representatives.

1.2.2   A Representative must be at least 25 years old, and a citizen of the United States for seven years. At the time he or she[3] is elected, the Representative must be a resident of the State that elected him or her.

1.2.3[4]   The number of Representatives that each State has will be based upon the population of each State. So will direct taxes (except for income tax[5]). For these purposes the population will count everybody except Indians who are not taxpayers. The right to vote may not be denied to any citizen in any State who is at least 18 years old.[6] This includes the right to vote for President and Vice President[7] of the United States, Representatives in Congress, as well as the Governor, judges and legislators of that State. If any State prevents or hinders any eligible person from voting, unless they participated in rebellion or other crime, the number of Representatives that State is entitled to will be reduced in proportion.

The actual Enumeration shall be made within three Years after the first Meeting of the Congress of the United States, and within every subsequent Term of ten Years, in such Manner as they shall by Law direct. The Number of Representatives shall not exceed one for every thirty Thousand, but each State shall have at Least one Representative; and until such enumeration shall be made, the State of New Hampshire shall be entitled to chuse three, Massachusetts eight, Rhode-Island and Providence Plantations one, Connecticut five, New-York six, New Jersey four, Pennsylvania eight, Delaware one, Maryland six, Virginia ten, North Carolina five, South Carolina five, and Georgia three.

When vacancies happen in the Representation from any State, the Executive Authority thereof shall issue Writs of Election to fill such Vacancies.

The House of Representatives shall chuse their Speaker and other Officers; and shall have the sole Power of Impeachment.

Section. 3.
The Senate of the United States shall be composed of two Senators from each State, chosen by the Legislature thereof for six Years; and each Senator shall have one Vote. [Changed by the 17th Amendment]

Immediately after they shall be assembled in Consequence of the first Election, they shall be divided as equally as may be into three Classes. The Seats of the Senators of the first Class shall be vacated at the Expiration of the second Year, of the second Class at the Expiration of the fourth Year, and of the third Class at the Expiration of the sixth Year, so that one third may be chosen every second Year;

and if Vacancies happen by Resignation, or otherwise, during the Recess of the Legislature of any State, the Executive thereof may make temporary Appointments until the next Meeting of the Legislature, which shall then fill such Vacancies. [Changed by the 17th Amendment]

The Constitution Made Easy

1.2.4   The actual census must be taken within three years after the first meeting of the Congress of the United States, and every ten years after that. Congress will determine by Law how the census will be taken. Each State will have at least one Representative, but otherwise not more than one for each 30,000 people.[8] Until the first census is taken the number of Representatives from each State will be New Hampshire three, Massachusetts eight, Rhode Island one, Connecticut five, New York six, New Jersey four, Pennsylvania eight, Delaware one, Maryland six, Virginia ten, North Carolina five, South Carolina five, and Georgia three.

1.2.5   When any Representative does not finish his or her term, the Governor from his or her State must appoint someone for the remainder of that term.

1.2.6   The House of Representatives will choose their Speaker and other officers, and will have the exclusive Power to bring a charge of Impeachment.[9]

Section 3
1.3.1[10] The Senate of the United States will consist of two Senators from each State, elected by the people of that State for six years; and each Senator will have one vote. Each State has a standard it uses to decide who is allowed to vote[11] for its own State legislature. This same standard must be used to determine who is allowed to vote for members of the Senate. [From A;17.1]

1.3.2   After the first election of Senators, and as soon they meet for the first time, they will be divided into three groups. The first term of the first group will end in two years; the first term of the second group will end in four years; and the first term of the third group will end in six years. In this way, one third of the Senate will be elected every two years.

1.3.3[12] When any Senator does not finish his or her term, the Governor from his or her State must set a Special Election to fill the remainder of that term. However, the legislature of that State may give the Governor power to make a temporary appointment that will only last until the position is filled by the Special Election. [From A;17.2]

No Person shall be a Senator who shall not have attained to the Age of thirty Years, and been nine Years a Citizen of the United States, and who shall not, when elected, be an Inhabitant of that State for which he shall be chosen.

The Vice President of the United States shall be President of the Senate, but shall have no Vote, unless they be equally divided.

The Senate shall chuse their other Officers, and also a President pro tempore, in the Absence of the Vice President, or when he shall exercise the Office of President of the United States.

The Senate shall have the sole Power to try all Impeachments. When sitting for that Purpose, they shall be on Oath or Affirmation. When the President of the United States is tried, the Chief Justice shall preside: And no Person shall be convicted without the Concurrence of two thirds of the Members present.

Judgment in Cases of Impeachment shall not extend further than to removal from Office, and disqualification to hold and enjoy any Office of honor, Trust or Profit under the United States: but the Party convicted shall nevertheless be liable and subject to Indictment, Trial, Judgment and Punishment, according to Law.

Section. 4.

The Times, Places and Manner of holding Elections for Senators and Representatives, shall be prescribed in each State by the Legislature thereof; but the Congress may at any time by Law make or alter such Regulations, except as to the Places of chusing Senators.

The Congress shall assemble at least once in every Year, and such Meeting shall be on the first Monday in December, unless they shall by Law appoint a different Day. [Changed by the 20th Amendment]

Section. 5.

Each House shall be the Judge of the Elections, Returns and Qualifications of its own Members, and a Majority of each shall constitute a Quorum to do Business; but a smaller Number may adjourn from day to day, and may be authorized to compel the Attendance of absent Members, in such Manner, and under such Penalties as each House may provide.

The Constitution Made Easy

1.3.4   A Senator must be at least 30 years old, and a citizen of the United States for nine years. At the time he or she is elected, the Senator must be a resident of the State that elected him or her.

1.3.5   The Vice President of the United States will be President[13] of the Senate, but may not vote except to break a tie.

1.3.6   The Senate will choose their other officers, and also a temporary[14] President. He or she will preside[15] only if the Vice President is absent, or when the Vice President is the Acting President of the United States.

1.3.7   The Senate will have the exclusive Power to try all Impeachments.[16] When they are conducting an Impeachment trial they must first swear that they will act impartially.[17] When the President of the United States is tried, the Chief Justice will preside. There will be no conviction unless two-thirds of the members present vote for it.

1.3.8   The most serious consequences of Impeachment will be to remove the person from office, and disqualify him or her from holding any official position under the United States. However, a convicted person may still have other liability, and could be charged, tried, judged and punished according to Law.[18]

Section 4
1.4.1   The times, places and methods of holding elections for Senators and Representatives, will be decided by each State legislature. Congress may override these regulations at any time by Law.[19]

1.4.2   The terms of Congress will end at Noon on January 3rd, and the terms of their successors will then begin. Congress must meet at least once in every year, and that meeting will also begin at Noon on January 3rd, unless that date is changed by Law.[20]

Section 5
1.5.1   Each House will decide its own elections, returns, and qualifications of its own members. Each House must have a majority present for there to be a quorum[21] that can do business. But a smaller number may meet and then adjourn[22] each day, and may be authorized to make the absent members attend. Each House may decide how members can be made to attend, or penalized for not attending.

Each House may determine the Rules of its Proceedings, punish its Members for disorderly Behaviour, and, with the Concurrence of two thirds, expel a Member.

Each House shall keep a Journal of its Proceedings, and from time to time publish the same, excepting such Parts as may in their Judgment require Secrecy; and the Yeas and Nays of the Members of either House on any question shall, at the Desire of one fifth of those Present, be entered on the Journal.

Neither House, during the Session of Congress, shall, without the Consent of the other, adjourn for more than three days, nor to any other Place than that in which the two Houses shall be sitting.

Section. 6.
The Senators and Representatives shall receive a Compensation for their Services, to be ascertained by Law, and paid out of the Treasury of the United States.

They shall in all Cases, except Treason, Felony and Breach of the Peace, be privileged from Arrest during their Attendance at the Session of their respective Houses, and in going to and returning from the same; and for any Speech or Debate in either House, they shall not be questioned in any other Place.

No Senator or Representative shall, during the Time for which he was elected, be appointed to any civil Office under the Authority of the United States, which shall have been created, or the Emoluments whereof shall have been encreased during such time; and no Person holding any Office under the United States, shall be a Member of either House during his Continuance in Office.

Section. 7.
All Bills for raising Revenue shall originate in the House of Representatives; but the Senate may propose or concur with Amendments as on other Bills.

Every Bill which shall have passed the House of Representatives and the Senate, shall, before it become a Law, be presented to the President of the United States: If he approve he shall sign it, but if not he shall return it, with his Objections to that House in which it shall have

The Constitution Made Easy

1.5.2   Each House may decide the rules of its proceedings, punish its members for disorderly conduct, and expel a member by a two-thirds vote.

1.5.3   Each House must keep a journal of its proceedings, and periodically publish it. They may omit certain parts that they believe require secrecy. One-fifth of those present in either House may require that the "Yes" and "No" votes of the members on any question be recorded in the journal.

1.5.4   When Congress is in session, neither House may adjourn for more than three days without the consent of the other House. The same consent will be required for either House to adjourn to any other location.

Section 6
1.6.1   Senators and Representatives must be paid for their services in an amount set by Law, and paid out of the Treasury of the United States. Any change in their pay will not take effect until after the next election of Representatives.[23]

1.6.2   They may not be arrested while they are attending a session of their respective Houses, or while they are going to or returning from a session, except for treason, felony or disturbing the peace.[24] They may not be arrested because of any speech or debate in either House, and they may not be questioned in any other place.

1.6.3   No Senator or Representative may be appointed to any official position under the authority of the United States during their term in office, if that position was created during their term, or if the pay plan was increased during their term. No person holding any official position under the United States may be a member of either House at the same time that he or she holds this other office.

Section 7
1.7.1   All bills for raising money must originate in the House of Representatives. But the Senate may propose or agree with amendments to these bills, just as it can with other bills.

1.7.2   Every bill which passes the House and Senate must be presented to the President of the United States before it becomes a Law. If the President approves of it, he or she must sign it. If not, the President must return it, along with his or her objections, to the House

originated, who shall enter the Objections at large on their Journal, and proceed to reconsider it.

If after such Reconsideration two thirds of that House shall agree to pass the Bill, it shall be sent, together with the Objections, to the other House, by which it shall likewise be reconsidered, and if approved by two thirds of that House, it shall become a Law.

But in all such Cases the Votes of both Houses shall be determined by yeas and Nays, and the Names of the Persons voting for and against the Bill shall be entered on the Journal of each House respectively. If any Bill shall not be returned by the President within ten Days (Sundays excepted) after it shall have been presented to him, the Same shall be a Law, in like Manner as if he had signed it, unless the Congress by their Adjournment prevent its Return, in which Case it shall not be a Law.

Every Order, Resolution, or Vote to which the Concurrence of the Senate and House of Representatives may be necessary (except on a question of Adjournment) shall be presented to the President of the United States; and before the Same shall take Effect, shall be approved by him, or being disapproved by him, shall be repassed by two thirds of the Senate and House of Representatives, according to the Rules and Limitations prescribed in the Case of a Bill.

Section. 8.
The Congress shall have Power

To lay and collect Taxes, Duties, Imposts and Excises, to pay the Debts and provide for the common Defence and general Welfare of the United States; but all Duties, Imposts and Excises shall be uniform throughout the United States;

To borrow Money on the credit of the United States;

To regulate Commerce with foreign Nations, and among the several States, and with the Indian Tribes;

To establish an uniform Rule of Naturalization, and uniform Laws on the subject of Bankruptcies throughout the United States;

in which it originated. That House must enter the President's objections on their journal, and proceed to reconsider it.

1.7.3   After they reconsider, if two-thirds of that House agrees to pass the bill, it must be sent, together with the objections, to the other House. That House must also reconsider it, and if they approve it by a two-thirds vote, it will become a Law.

1.7.4   In all such cases the votes of both Houses must be determined by saying "Yes" or "No," and the names of the people voting for and against the bill must be entered on the journal of each House respectively. If any bill is not returned by the President within ten days after it has been presented to him or her (not counting Sundays), it will become a Law, just as if he or she had signed it. There is an exception if Congress adjourns in less than ten days, which prevents its return, in which case it will not become Law.

1.7.5   Every other kind of order, resolution, or vote which the Senate and House of Representatives have to both agree on, must be presented to the President of the United States. Before it can take effect, it must be approved by him or her. If the President does not approve it, it must be re-passed by two-thirds of the Senate and House of Representatives in order for it to go into effect. The same rules and limitations apply as in the case of a bill (above). This paragraph does not apply to a vote to adjourn.

Section 8
Congress will have Power:

1.8.1   To assess and collect taxes on imports, exports, and purchases to pay the debts and provide for the common defense and general well-being[25] of the United States. All such taxes must be uniform[26] throughout the United States;

1.8.2   To borrow money on the credit of the United States;

1.8.3   To regulate trade with foreign nations, and among the separate States, and with the Indian tribes;

1.8.4   To establish standard rules for becoming a naturalized citizen,[27] and establish standard Laws about bankruptcy throughout the United States;

To coin Money, regulate the Value thereof, and of foreign Coin, and fix the Standard of Weights and Measures;

To provide for the Punishment of counterfeiting the Securities and current Coin of the United States;

To establish Post Offices and post Roads;

To promote the Progress of Science and useful Arts, by securing for limited Times to Authors and Inventors the exclusive Right to their respective Writings and Discoveries;

To constitute Tribunals inferior to the supreme Court;

To define and punish Piracies and Felonies committed on the high Seas, and Offences against the Law of Nations;

To declare War, grant Letters of Marque and Reprisal, and make Rules concerning Captures on Land and Water;

To raise and support Armies, but no Appropriation of Money to that Use shall be for a longer Term than two Years;

To provide and maintain a Navy;

To make Rules for the Government and Regulation of the land and naval Forces;

To provide for calling forth the Militia to execute the Laws of the Union, suppress Insurrections and repel Invasions;

To provide for organizing, arming, and disciplining, the Militia, and for governing such Part of them as may be employed in the Service of the United States, reserving to the States respectively, the Appointment of the Officers, and the Authority of training the Militia according to the discipline prescribed by Congress;

To exercise exclusive Legislation in all Cases whatsoever, over such District (not exceeding ten Miles square) as may, by Cession of particular States, and the Acceptance of Congress, become the Seat of the Government of the United States, and to exercise like Authority over all Places purchased by the Consent of the Legislature of the State in

The Constitution Made Easy

1.8.5   To coin money, decide the value of it, decide the value of foreign money, and set the standard of weights and measures;

1.8.6   To decide the punishment for counterfeiting the money and other valuables of the United States;

1.8.7   To establish post offices and post roads;

1.8.8   To promote the progress of science and useful arts, by making sure that authors and inventors have ownership of their writings and discoveries for a certain period of time;

1.8.9   To create courts underneath the Supreme Court;

1.8.10 To define and punish piracy, felonies committed on the high seas, and international crimes;

1.8.11 To declare war, grant letters of retaliation,[28] and make rules concerning captures[29] on land and water;

1.8.12 To raise and support Armies. But Congress may not allocate money for this purpose for more than two years at a time;

1.8.13 To provide and maintain a Navy;

1.8.14 To make rules that govern and regulate the land and naval forces;

1.8.15 To provide for calling upon the Militia[30] to enforce the Laws of the Union, put down rebellions and repel invasions;

1.8.16 To provide for organizing, arming, and disciplining the Militia, and for governing any part of them that are serving the United States at the time. The States will still appoint the officers, and have the authority to train the Militia according to the standards prescribed by Congress;

1.8.17 To make all Laws whatsoever for the District that will be the headquarters of the Government of the United States (Washington, D.C.).[31] This District will not be more than ten miles square, and will consist of land granted by one or more States and accepted by Congress. Congress will have the same authority over forts, storage places for weapons and ammunition, dock-yards[32] and other

which the Same shall be, for the Erection of Forts, Magazines, Arsenals, dock-Yards, and other needful Buildings;--And

To make all Laws which shall be necessary and proper for carrying into Execution the foregoing Powers, and all other Powers vested by this Constitution in the Government of the United States, or in any Department or Officer thereof.

Section. 9.

The Migration or Importation of such Persons as any of the States now existing shall think proper to admit, shall not be prohibited by the Congress prior to the Year one thousand eight hundred and eight, but a Tax or duty may be imposed on such Importation, not exceeding ten dollars for each Person.

The Privilege of the Writ of Habeas Corpus shall not be suspended, unless when in Cases of Rebellion or Invasion the public Safety may require it.

No Bill of Attainder or ex post facto Law shall be passed.

No Capitation, or other direct, Tax shall be laid, <u>unless in Proportion to the Census or enumeration herein before directed to be taken</u>. [Changed by the 16th Amendment]

No Tax or Duty shall be laid on Articles exported from any State.

No Preference shall be given by any Regulation of Commerce or Revenue to the Ports of one State over those of another; nor shall Vessels bound to, or from, one State, be obliged to enter, clear, or pay Duties in another.

No Money shall be drawn from the Treasury, but in Consequence of Appropriations made by Law; and a regular Statement and Account of the Receipts and Expenditures of all public Money shall be published from time to time.

No Title of Nobility shall be granted by the United States: And no Person holding any Office of Profit or Trust under them, shall, without the Consent of the Congress, accept of any present, Emolument, Office, or Title, of any kind whatever, from any King, Prince, or foreign State.

necessary buildings. These places must first be purchased with the consent of the legislature of the State where they are located; and

1.8.18 To make all Laws which are necessary and proper for executing the Powers listed above, and all other Powers granted by this Constitution to the Government of the United States, or to any department or officer of it.

Section 9[33]

1.9.1 The existing States may allow any people they wish to be admitted or imported. Congress may not prohibit this before the year 1808, but may impose a tax of up to ten dollars per person. [This clause was changed by Law on January 1, 1808.[34]]

1.9.2 The right of any arrested person to be seen by an impartial judge[35] may not be suspended. There may be exceptions only during a rebellion or invasion if the public safety requires it.

1.9.3 No Law may be passed which pronounces a person guilty of a crime,[36] or which is retroactive.[37]

1.9.4 No direct taxes may be assessed unless they are in proportion to the census. There is an exception for income tax.[38]

1.9.5 No tax may be assessed on goods exported from any State.

1.9.6 No preference may be given to the ports of one State over those of another by regulating the trade or taxes. Ships bound to or from one State, may not be required to enter, stop at, or pay taxes in another.

1.9.7 No money may be taken out of the Treasury, except the amounts that have been allocated by Law. A financial statement showing where this money came from, and how it was spent, must be made available to the public on a regular basis.

1.9.8 No title of nobility may be granted by the United States.[39] No person who holds any official position under them may accept any gift, money, office, or title of any kind whatever; from any king, prince or foreign State, without the consent of Congress.

Section. 10.

No State shall enter into any Treaty, Alliance, or Confederation; grant Letters of Marque and Reprisal;

coin Money; emit Bills of Credit; make any Thing but gold and silver Coin a Tender in Payment of Debts;

pass any Bill of Attainder, ex post facto Law,

or Law impairing the Obligation of Contracts, or grant any Title of Nobility.

No State shall, without the Consent of the Congress, lay any Imposts or Duties on Imports or Exports, except what may be absolutely necessary for executing it's inspection Laws: and the net Produce of all Duties and Imposts, laid by any State on Imports or Exports, shall be for the Use of the Treasury of the United States; and all such Laws shall be subject to the Revision and Controul of the Congress.

No State shall, without the Consent of Congress, lay any Duty of Tonnage, keep Troops, or Ships of War in time of Peace, enter into any Agreement or Compact with another State, or with a foreign Power, or engage in War, unless actually invaded, or in such imminent Danger as will not admit of delay.

Article. II.

Section. 1.

The executive Power shall be vested in a President of the United States of America. He shall hold his Office during the Term of four Years, and, together with the Vice President, chosen for the same Term, be elected, as follows:

Each State shall appoint, in such Manner as the Legislature thereof may direct, a Number of Electors, equal to the whole Number of Senators and Representatives to which the State may be entitled in the Congress: but no Senator or Representative, or Person holding an Office of Trust or Profit under the United States, shall be appointed an Elector.

The Constitution Made Easy

Section 10[40]

1.10.1 No State may enter into any treaty, alliance, or confederation; or grant letters of retaliation.[41]

1.10.2 (No State may) coin money, print paper money, or make anything except gold and silver coin a method of paying debts.

1.10.3 (No State may) pass any Law which pronounces a person guilty of a crime,[42] or which is retroactive.[43]

1.10.4 (No State may) pass any Law that interferes with private contracts, or grant any title of nobility.

1.10.5 The consent of Congress is required before any State may assess any tax on imports or exports, except what is absolutely necessary for executing it's inspection Laws. The net proceeds of all these taxes will be for the use of the Treasury of the United States, and all such Laws will be subject to the revision and control of Congress.

1.10.6 The consent of Congress is required before any State may assess any tax based on the weight of shipments, or keep troops or warships in time of peace, or enter into any agreement or compact with another State or foreign Power, or engage in war. There is an exception for engaging in war if a State is actually invaded, or is in such immediate danger that it does not dare to wait.

Article 2

Section 1

2.1.1 The executive Power will be entrusted to a President of the United States of America. He or she will hold his or her office for a term of four years, not to exceed two terms.[44] Each term will begin and end at Noon on January 20th.[45] The President and Vice President will be elected to the same term as follows:

2.1.2 Each State, (and Washington, D.C.[46]), must appoint a number of electors equal to the total number of Senators and Representatives which that State (or District) is entitled to in Congress. The legislature of each State may determine the manner in which the electors are chosen. No Senator or Representative, or person holding an official position under the United States, may be appointed as an elector.

The Electors shall meet in their respective States, and vote by Ballot for two Persons, of whom one at least shall not be an Inhabitant of the same State with themselves. [Changed by the 12th Amendment]

And they shall make a List of all the Persons voted for, and of the Number of Votes for each; which List they shall sign and certify, and transmit sealed to the Seat of the Government of the United States, directed to the President of the Senate. [Changed by the 12th Amendment]

The President of the Senate shall, in the Presence of the Senate and House of Representatives, open all the Certificates, and the Votes shall then be counted. The Person having the greatest Number of Votes shall be the President, if such Number be a Majority of the whole Number of Electors appointed; [Changed by the 12th Amendment]

and if there be more than one who have such Majority, and have an equal Number of Votes, then the House of Representatives shall immediately chuse by Ballot one of them for President; and if no Person have a Majority, then from the five highest on the List the said House shall in like Manner chuse the President. But in chusing the President, the Votes shall be taken by States, the Representation from each State having one Vote; A quorum for this purpose shall consist of a Member or Members from two thirds of the States, and a Majority of all the States shall be necessary to a Choice. [Changed by the 12th Amendment]

[See Section 3 of Amendment 20]

[See Section 3 of Amendment 20]

The Constitution Made Easy

2.1.3[47] The electors must meet in their respective States, and vote by ballot for President and Vice President. They may not vote for a President and a Vice President who are both from the same State as the electors. [From A:12.1]

2.1.4 They must name in one set of ballots the person they voted for as President, and in a different set of ballots the person they voted for as Vice President. They must make separate lists of all the persons they voted for as President, and of all persons they voted for as Vice President, and the number of votes for each. They must sign these lists, and certify that they are correct, and send them sealed to the President of the Senate. [From A:12.2]

2.1.5 The President of the Senate must open all the certificates in the presence of the Senate and House of Representatives, and the votes must then be counted. The person receiving the greatest number of votes for President will become the President, as long as he or she receives a majority of the total number of electors. [From A:12.3]

2.1.6 If no person receives a majority, then the House of Representatives must immediately elect the President by ballot. They must choose him or her from the three persons with the highest numbers of votes. In choosing the President, the votes must be taken by States, and each State will have one vote. A quorum for this purpose will consist of at least one member from two-thirds of the States, and a majority of all the States will be necessary for the election to be final. [From A:12.4]

2.1.7 If the President elect dies before the beginning of his or her term (Noon, January 20th), then the Vice President elect will become President. If a President has not been chosen before the beginning of his or her term, or if the President elect does not qualify, then the Vice President elect will act as President until a qualified President is chosen. [From A:12.5 and A:20.3.1]

2.1.8 In case neither a President elect, nor a Vice President elect qualifies, Congress may provide for this by law. Then this law will determine who will act as President, or the way in which the Acting President will be selected. This person will act as President until a qualified President or Vice President is chosen. [From A:12.6 and A:20.3.2]

In every Case, after the Choice of the President, the Person having the greatest Number of Votes of the Electors shall be the Vice President. But if there should remain two or more who have equal Votes, the Senate shall chuse from them by Ballot the Vice President. [Changed by the 12th Amendment]

The Congress may determine the Time of chusing the Electors, and the Day on which they shall give their Votes; which Day shall be the same throughout the United States.

No Person except a natural born Citizen, or a Citizen of the United States, at the time of the Adoption of this Constitution, shall be eligible to the Office of President; neither shall any Person be eligible to that Office who shall not have attained to the Age of thirty five Years, and been fourteen Years a Resident within the United States.

In Case of the Removal of the President from Office, or of his Death, Resignation, or Inability to discharge the Powers and Duties of the said Office, the Same shall devolve on the Vice President, [Changed by the 25th Amendment]

[See Amendment 25]

and the Congress may by Law provide for the Case of Removal, Death, Resignation or Inability, both of the President and Vice President, declaring what Officer shall then act as President, and such Officer shall act accordingly, until the Disability be removed, or a President shall be elected. [*The whole paragraph (above) was underlined in the original; but a portion has been retained in this version as there is no replacement language in the 25th Amendment, or any other Amendment. See 2.1.14 and footnote.]

[See Amendment 25]

The Constitution Made Easy

2.1.9 The person receiving the greatest number of votes for Vice President will become the Vice President, as long as he or she receives a majority of the total number of electors. If no person receives a majority, then the Senate must choose the Vice President from the two persons with the highest numbers of votes. A quorum for this purpose will consist of two-thirds of the total number of Senators, and a majority of the total number will be necessary for the election to be final. If a person is not eligible, under the Constitution, to be President of the United States, that person will not be eligible to be Vice President either. [From A:12.7]

2.1.10 Congress may determine the time of choosing the electors, and the day on which they must cast their votes. This day must be the same throughout the United States.

2.1.11 To be eligible for the office of President, a person must be a natural-born citizen (or else a citizen at the time this Constitution was adopted). He or she must also be at least 35 years old and a resident within the United States for fourteen years.

2.1.12[48] In case of the removal of the President from office, or of his or her death or resignation, the Vice President will become President. [From A:25.1]

2.1.13 Whenever there is a vacancy in the office of the Vice President, the President must nominate a new Vice President. He will take office upon confirmation by a majority vote of both Houses of Congress. [From A:25.2]

2.1.14 In case the President and Vice President are both removed from office, or have died, or have resigned, or have become unable to discharge the powers and duties of office, Congress may provide for this by law. Then this law will determine who will act as President until one of them is able to resume their office, or until a new President is elected.[49]

2.1.15 Whenever the President believes that he or she is unable to discharge the powers and duties of office, he or she may send written declaration to the temporary President of the Senate and to the Speaker of the House of Representatives. Until the President sends them a written declaration that he or she has become able again, these powers and duties must be discharged by the Vice President as Acting President. [From A:25.3]

[See Amendment 25]

[See Amendment 25]

[See Amendment 25]

The President shall, at stated Times, receive for his Services, a Compensation, which shall neither be increased nor diminished during the Period for which he shall have been elected, and he shall not receive within that Period any other Emolument from the United States, or any of them.

Before he enter on the Execution of his Office, he shall take the following Oath or Affirmation:--"I do solemnly swear (or affirm) that I will faithfully execute the Office of President of the United States, and will to the best of my Ability, preserve, protect and defend the Constitution of the United States."

2.1.16 Whenever the Vice President and a majority of the Cabinet officers[50] agree that the President is unable to discharge the powers and duties of office, they may send their written declaration to the temporary President of the Senate and the Speaker of the House of Representatives. Then the Vice President must immediately assume the powers and duties as Acting President. (Congress may change this in the future from "the Cabinet" to some other group they designate by law.) [From A:25.4]

2.1.17 After this, if the President believes that no inability exists, he or she must send written declaration to the temporary President of the Senate and to the Speaker of the House of Representatives. The President will resume the powers and duties of office unless the Vice President and a majority of the Cabinet officers oppose him or her. If they do, they must send their written declaration within four days to the temporary President of the Senate and to the Speaker of the House of Representatives reasserting that the President is unable to discharge the powers and duties of office. [From A:25.5]

2.1.18 At this point Congress must decide the issue. They must meet within 48 hours for this purpose if they are not already in session. Congress must make a determination within 21 days of receiving the most recent declaration (or 23 days if they were not in session). If Congress determines that the President is unable to discharge the powers and duties of office, then the Vice President will continue as Acting President. They must do this by two-thirds vote of both Houses. Otherwise, the President will resume the powers and duties of his or her office. [From A:25.6]

2.1.19 The President must be paid on a regular basis. This pay may not be increased nor decreased during his or her term in office. During this term, the President may not receive any other payment from the United States, or any of them.

2.1.20 Before the President actually exercises any of the powers or duties of office, he or she must take the following Oath or Affirmation: "I do solemnly swear (or affirm) that I will faithfully execute the office of President of the United States, and will to the best of my ability, preserve, protect and defend the Constitution of the United States."

Section. 2.

The President shall be Commander in Chief of the Army and Navy of the United States, and of the Militia of the several States, when called into the actual Service of the United States; he may require the Opinion, in writing, of the principal Officer in each of the executive Departments, upon any Subject relating to the Duties of their respective Offices, and he shall have Power to grant Reprieves and Pardons for Offences against the United States, except in Cases of Impeachment.

He shall have Power, by and with the Advice and Consent of the Senate, to make Treaties, provided two thirds of the Senators present concur; and he shall nominate, and by and with the Advice and Consent of the Senate, shall appoint Ambassadors, other public Ministers and Consuls, Judges of the supreme Court, and all other Officers of the United States, whose Appointments are not herein otherwise provided for, and which shall be established by Law:

but the Congress may by Law vest the Appointment of such inferior Officers, as they think proper, in the President alone, in the Courts of Law, or in the Heads of Departments.

The President shall have Power to fill up all Vacancies that may happen during the Recess of the Senate, by granting Commissions which shall expire at the End of their next Session.

Section. 3.

He shall from time to time give to the Congress Information of the State of the Union, and recommend to their Consideration such Measures as he shall judge necessary and expedient;

he may, on extraordinary Occasions, convene both Houses, or either of them, and in Case of Disagreement between them, with Respect to the Time of Adjournment, he may adjourn them to such Time as he shall think proper;

he shall receive Ambassadors and other public Ministers; he shall take Care that the Laws be faithfully executed, and shall Commission all the Officers of the United States.

The Constitution Made Easy

Section 2

2.2.1   The President will be Commander in Chief of the Army and Navy of the United States, and of the Militia of the separate States, when they are called into the actual service of the United States. The President may require the written opinion of the Cabinet officers upon any subject relating to the duties of their respective offices. He or she will have Power to grant reprieves and pardons for offenses against the United States, except in cases of Impeachment.

2.2.2   The President will have Power to make treaties with the advice and consent of the Senate. Two-thirds of the Senators present must agree. He or she must nominate and then appoint ambassadors, public officials, diplomats, Judges of the Supreme Court, and all other officers of the United States. This includes any appointments that are not provided for elsewhere in the Constitution, but are later established by Law. These appointments also require the advice and consent of the Senate.

2.2.3   But Congress may give the President the Power to appoint some lower-ranking officers by himself or herself. Congress may give the same power to the courts of Law, or the heads of departments. They would do this by Law, as they think it is proper.

2.2.4   The President will have Power to fill up all vacancies that may happen during the recess of the Senate, by granting commissions which will expire at the end of their next session.

Section 3

2.3.1   The President must regularly give information to Congress concerning the State of the Union, and recommend for their consideration whatever measures he or she thinks are necessary and expedient.

2.3.2   On extraordinary occasions, the President may convene one or both Houses of Congress. In cases when the two Houses disagree about when to adjourn, the President may adjourn them to the time he or she thinks is proper.

2.3.3   The President must receive ambassadors and other public officials. He or she must make sure that the Laws are faithfully carried out, and must commission all the officers of the United States.

Section. 4.

The President, Vice President and all civil Officers of the United States, shall be removed from Office on Impeachment for, and Conviction of, Treason, Bribery, or other high Crimes and Misdemeanors.

Article III.

Section. 1.

The judicial Power of the United States shall be vested in one supreme Court, and in such inferior Courts as the Congress may from time to time ordain and establish. The Judges, both of the supreme and inferior Courts, shall hold their Offices during good Behaviour, and shall, at stated Times, receive for their Services a Compensation, which shall not be diminished during their Continuance in Office.

Section. 2.

The judicial Power shall extend to all Cases, in Law and Equity, arising under this Constitution, the Laws of the United States, and Treaties made, or which shall be made, under their Authority;--to all Cases affecting Ambassadors, other public Ministers and Consuls;--to all Cases of admiralty and maritime Jurisdiction;--to Controversies to which the United States shall be a Party;--to Controversies between two or more States;-- between a State and Citizens of another State;--between Citizens of different States;--between Citizens of the same State claiming Lands under Grants of different States, and between a State, or the Citizens thereof, and foreign States, Citizens or Subjects. [Changed by the 11th Amendment.]

In all Cases affecting Ambassadors, other public Ministers and Consuls, and those in which a State shall be Party, the supreme Court shall have original Jurisdiction. In all the other Cases before mentioned, the supreme Court shall have appellate Jurisdiction, both as to Law and Fact, with such Exceptions, and under such Regulations as the Congress shall make.

The Trial of all Crimes, except in Cases of Impeachment, shall be by Jury; and such Trial shall be held in the State where the said Crimes shall have been committed; but when not committed within any State, the Trial shall be at such Place or Places as the Congress may by Law have directed.

The Constitution Made Easy

Section 4

    The President, Vice President and all government officials of the United States, must be removed from office if they are Impeached for, and then convicted of, treason, bribery, or other felonies or misdemeanors.

<u>Article 3</u>

Section 1

    The judicial Power of the United States, will be entrusted to one Supreme Court, and in whatever lower courts Congress decides to create in the future. The Judges of all these courts may stay in office for as long as they demonstrate good behavior. They must be paid for their services on a regular basis, and their pay may not be decreased during their time in office.

Section 2

3.2.1   The judicial Power will include all civil and criminal cases that concern this Constitution, the Laws of the United States, and treaties made under their authority. The judicial Power will also include all cases affecting ambassadors, other public officers and diplomats, and all cases where the Laws of the oceans and seas apply. The judicial Power will also include all controversies in which the United States is one of the parties, all controversies between two or more States, between citizens of different States, and between citizens of the same State who are claiming lands under grants of different States.[51]

3.2.2   The Supreme Court will have primary authority over all cases that affect ambassadors, other public officials and diplomats, and those cases in which a State is involved. The Supreme Court will have authority in all of the other cases previously mentioned if the cases are appealed to them. This authority will include both matters of Law and fact. There may be exceptions under regulations that Congress makes.

3.2.3   Trials for all crimes, except cases of Impeachment, must be by jury; and these trials must be held in the State where the crimes were committed. If the crimes were not committed inside of any State, the trial will be held wherever Congress has decided by Law.

Section. 3.

Treason against the United States, shall consist only in levying War against them, or in adhering to their Enemies, giving them Aid and Comfort. No Person shall be convicted of Treason unless on the Testimony of two Witnesses to the same overt Act, or on Confession in open Court.

The Congress shall have Power to declare the Punishment of Treason, but no Attainder of Treason shall work Corruption of Blood, or Forfeiture except during the Life of the Person attainted.

Article. IV.

Section. 1.

Full Faith and Credit shall be given in each State to the public Acts, Records, and judicial Proceedings of every other State. And the Congress may by general Laws prescribe the Manner in which such Acts, Records and Proceedings shall be proved, and the Effect thereof.

Section. 2.

The Citizens of each State shall be entitled to all Privileges and Immunities of Citizens in the several States.

A Person charged in any State with Treason, Felony, or other Crime, who shall flee from Justice, and be found in another State, shall on Demand of the executive Authority of the State from which he fled, be delivered up, to be removed to the State having Jurisdiction of the Crime.

No Person held to Service or Labour in one State, under the Laws thereof, escaping into another, shall, in Consequence of any Law or Regulation therein, be discharged from such Service or Labour, but shall be delivered up on Claim of the Party to whom such Service or Labour may be due. [Changed by the 13th Amendment]

Section. 3.

New States may be admitted by the Congress into this Union; but no new State shall be formed or erected within the Jurisdiction of any other State; nor any State be formed by the Junction of two or more States, or Parts of States, without the Consent of the Legislatures of the States concerned as well as of the Congress.

The Constitution Made Easy

Section 3
3.3.1   Treason against the United States means making war against them, or joining with their enemies, or giving them assistance and support. A person may not be convicted of treason unless there is testimony of at least two witnesses to the same actual act, or unless the person confesses in a public courtroom.

3.3.2   Congress will have Power to declare the punishment for treason, but the penalty may not include confiscating a person's property after that person is executed.[52]

Article 4

Section 1
   Each State must fully accept the public acts, records, and court actions of every other State. Congress may write general Laws[53] that describe how these acts, records and court actions can be proven, and what effect they will have.

Section 2
4.2.1   The citizens of each State will be entitled to all the privileges and freedoms of citizens in the other States.

4.2.2   If a person is charged with treason, felony, or other crime in one State, then flees to another State and is found there, then this fugitive must be returned to the State he or she fled from, if the executive authority from that State demands it.

[Made obsolete by the 13th Amendment[54]]

Section 3
4.3.1   New States may be admitted into this Union by Congress. But no new State may be formed or created within the boundaries of any other State unless it is approved by Congress and the legislature of the State affected. And no new State may be formed by combining two or more States, or parts of those States, unless it is approved by Congress and the legislatures of the States affected.

The Congress shall have Power to dispose of and make all needful Rules and Regulations respecting the Territory or other Property belonging to the United States; and nothing in this Constitution shall be so construed as to Prejudice any Claims of the United States, or of any particular State.

Section. 4.

The United States shall guarantee to every State in this Union a Republican Form of Government, and shall protect each of them against Invasion; and on Application of the Legislature, or of the Executive (when the Legislature cannot be convened), against domestic Violence.

Article. V.

The Congress, whenever two thirds of both Houses shall deem it necessary, shall propose Amendments to this Constitution, or, on the Application of the Legislatures of two thirds of the several States, shall call a Convention for proposing Amendments,

which, in either Case, shall be valid to all Intents and Purposes, as Part of this Constitution, when ratified by the Legislatures of three fourths of the several States, or by Conventions in three fourths thereof, as the one or the other Mode of Ratification may be proposed by the Congress;

Provided that no Amendment which may be made prior to the Year One thousand eight hundred and eight shall in any Manner affect the first and fourth Clauses in the Ninth Section of the first Article; and that no State, without its Consent, shall be deprived of its equal Suffrage in the Senate.

4.3.2   Congress will have Power to sell or transfer the territory or other property belonging to the United States, and to make all necessary rules and regulations for them. But nothing in this Constitution may be interpreted in a way that it gives any State, or the United States, any preference concerning claims they may have.

Section 4

The United States will guarantee a Republican form of Government to every State in this Union, and will protect each of them from invasion. They will also be protected from domestic violence if the legislature of a State requests it. If the legislature cannot be convened, the Governor of that State may request it.

Article 5

Section 1

Amendments to this Constitution may be proposed in two different ways. The first way is for Congress to propose them whenever two-thirds of both Houses decide it is necessary. The second way is for the legislatures of two-thirds of the States to request it, and then Congress must call a convention for proposing Amendments.

Section 2

There are also two different ways for the proposed Amendments to receive final approval[55] and Congress will propose one. The first way is for three-fourths of the State legislatures to approve them. The second way is for conventions in three-fourths of the States to approve them. If they are approved, these Amendments will become an actual part of the Constitution.

Section 3

No Amendment may be made before the year 1808 which affects **C:1.9.1 or 1.9.4** of this Constitution in any way. No State may ever be deprived of equal representation in the Senate without its consent.

Article. VI.

All Debts contracted and Engagements entered into, before the Adoption of this Constitution, shall be as valid against the United States under this Constitution, as under the Confederation.

This Constitution, and the Laws of the United States which shall be made in Pursuance thereof; and all Treaties made, or which shall be made, under the Authority of the United States, shall be the supreme Law of the Land; and the Judges in every State shall be bound thereby, any Thing in the Constitution or Laws of any State to the Contrary notwithstanding.

The Senators and Representatives before mentioned, and the Members of the several State Legislatures, and all executive and judicial Officers, both of the United States and of the several States, shall be bound by Oath or Affirmation, to support this Constitution; but no religious Test shall ever be required as a Qualification to any Office or public Trust under the United States.

Article. VII.

The Ratification of the Conventions of nine States, shall be sufficient for the Establishment of this Constitution between the States so ratifying the Same.

Done in Convention by the Unanimous Consent of the States present the Seventeenth Day of September in the Year of our Lord one thousand seven hundred and Eighty seven and of the Independence of the United States of America the Twelfth In witness whereof We have hereunto subscribed our Names,

G . Washington--President and deputy from Virginia

Attest William Jackson Secretary

Delaware   Geo: Read, Gunning Bedford jun, John Dickinson, Richard Bassett Jaco: Broom

The Constitution Made Easy

Article 6

Section 1

All debts that have been incurred, and all agreements that have been made, before this Constitution becomes effective, will be just as binding upon the United States under this Constitution, as they were under the Confederation.[56]

Section 2

This Constitution will be the supreme Law of the land. So are the Laws of the United States which are made that conform with it. So are all treaties made by the authority of the United States in the past, and in the future. Judges in every State will be bound by them. Nothing in any State Law or State Constitution which is different may stand against them.

Section 3

All Senators and Representatives, and every member of every State legislature, and all executive and judicial officers of the United States, and of every State, will be bound by Oath or Affirmation, to support this Constitution. But no religious test may ever be required as a qualification for any official position under the United States.

Article 7

Approval by the Conventions of nine States will be enough for establishing this Constitution between the States that approve it.

This has been done in convention, by the unanimous consent of the States who are present, on September 17th, in the Year of our Lord 1787, which is also the twelfth year of the Independence of the United States of America. As witnesses of this we have signed our Names as follows:

George Washington--President and deputy from Virginia

Attest William Jackson Secretary

Delaware: George Read, Gunning Bedford, Jr., John Dickinson, Richard Bassett, Jacob Broom

Maryland	James McHenry, Dan of St Thos. Jenifer, Danl Carroll
Virginia	John Blair, James Madison Jr.
North Carolina	Wm. Blount, Richd. Dobbs Spaight, Hu Williamson
South Carolina	J. Rutledge, Charles Cotesworth Pinckney, Charles Pinckney, Pierce Butler
Georgia	William Few, Abr Baldwin
New Hampshire	John Langdon, Nicholas Gilman
Massachusetts	Nathaniel Gorham, Rufus King
Connecticut	Wm. Saml. Johnson, Roger Sherman
New York	Alexander Hamilton
New Jersey	Wil: Livingston, David Brearley, Wm. Paterson, Jona: Dayton
Pennsylvania	B Franklin, Thomas Mifflin, Robt Morris, Geo. Clymer, Thos. FitzSimons, Jared Ingersoll, James Wilson, Gouv Morris

Text of Constitution taken from:
http://www.archives.gov/exhibits/charters/constitution_transcript.html
Retrieved August 3, 2011

The Constitution Made Easy

Maryland: James McHenry, Daniel of St. Thomas Jenifer, Daniel Carroll

Virginia: John Blair, James Madison Jr.

North Carolina: William Blount, Richard Dobbs Spaight, Hugh Williamson

South Carolina: John Rutledge, Charles Cotesworth Pinckney, Charles Pinckney, Pierce Butler

Georgia: William Few, Abraham Baldwin

New Hampshire: John Langdon, Nicholas Gilman

Massachusetts: Nathaniel Gorham, Rufus King

Connecticut: William Samuel Johnson, Roger Sherman

New York: Alexander Hamilton

New Jersey: William Livingston, David Brearley, William Paterson, Jonathan Dayton

Pennsylvania: Benjamin Franklin, Thomas Mifflin, Robert Morris, George Clymer, Thomas FitzSimons, Jared Ingersoll, James Wilson, Gouvernor Morris

The Constitution of the United States

The Bill of Rights

Preamble

Congress of the United States
begun and held at the City of New-York, on
Wednesday the fourth of March, one thousand seven hundred and eighty nine.

THE Conventions of a number of the States, having at the time of their adopting the Constitution, expressed a desire, in order to prevent misconstruction or abuse of its powers, that further declaratory and restrictive clauses should be added: And as extending the ground of public confidence in the Government, will best ensure the beneficent ends of its institution.

RESOLVED by the Senate and House of Representatives of the United States of America, in Congress assembled, two thirds of both Houses concurring, that the following Articles be proposed to the Legislatures of the several States, as amendments to the Constitution of the United States, all, or any of which Articles, when ratified by three fourths of the said Legislatures, to be valid to all intents and purposes, as part of the said Constitution; viz.

ARTICLES in addition to, and Amendment of the Constitution of the United States of America, proposed by Congress, and ratified by the Legislatures of the several States, pursuant to the fifth Article of the original Constitution.

Note: The following text is a transcription of the first ten amendments to the Constitution in their original form. These amendments were ratified December 15, 1791, and form what is known as the "Bill of Rights."

Amendment I

Congress shall make no law respecting an establishment of religion, or prohibiting the free exercise thereof; or abridging the freedom of speech, or of the press; or the right of the people peaceably to assemble, and to petition the Government for a redress of grievances.

The Constitution Made Easy

The Bill of Rights[57]

Preamble

(The following is presented by the) Congress of the United States, which convened in New York City on Wednesday, March 4, 1789.

At the time that they adopted the Constitution, several of the State Conventions expressed a desire that further declarations and restrictions should be added in order to prevent misinterpretation or abuse of the Constitution's powers. Since doing so will increase the basis for public confidence in the Government, and is the best way to make sure that the results of establishing it are beneficial;

It is RESOLVED by the Senate and the House of Representatives of the United States of America, while assembled in Congress, and agreed to by two-thirds of both Houses, that the following Articles are to be proposed to the legislatures of the various States. Any of these Articles that are approved by three-fourths of the State legislatures will become Amendments to the Constitution, and will become valid as an actual part of the Constitution.

The following ARTICLES are in addition to, and Amendments of, the Constitution of the United States of America. They have been proposed by Congress and approved by the legislatures of the various States, as required by Article Five of the original Constitution.

Amendment 1

Congress may not make any law that sets up any religion, or interferes with any religious practice. Congress may not make any law that diminishes the freedom of speech, or the freedom of the press, or the right of the people to assemble peacefully, or the right of the people to petition the Government to make things right if it has caused them harm.

Amendment II

A well regulated Militia, being necessary to the security of a free State, the right of the people to keep and bear Arms, shall not be infringed.

Amendment III

No Soldier shall, in time of peace be quartered in any house, without the consent of the Owner, nor in time of war, but in a manner to be prescribed by law.

Amendment IV

The right of the people to be secure in their persons, houses, papers, and effects, against unreasonable searches and seizures, shall not be violated, and no Warrants shall issue, but upon probable cause, supported by Oath or affirmation, and particularly describing the place to be searched, and the persons or things to be seized.

Amendment V

No person shall be held to answer for a capital, or otherwise infamous crime, unless on a presentment or indictment of a Grand Jury, except in cases arising in the land or naval forces, or in the Militia, when in actual service in time of War or public danger;

nor shall any person be subject for the same offence to be twice put in jeopardy of life or limb; nor shall be compelled in any criminal case to be a witness against himself, nor be deprived of life, liberty, or property, without due process of law; nor shall private property be taken for public use, without just compensation.

The Constitution Made Easy

Amendment 2

The people have the right to own and carry firearms,[58] and it may not be violated because a well-equipped Militia[59] is necessary for a State to remain secure and free.

Amendment 3

Soldiers may not be housed in private homes in peacetime unless the owner gives his consent. Soldiers may only be housed in private homes in wartime in a way that will be described by law.

Amendment 4

The people have the right to be protected from unreasonable searches and seizures, and it may not be violated. This protection includes their persons, houses, papers and belongings. No warrant may be issued unless it is reasonably believed that a crime was most likely committed.[60] This belief must be supported by a sworn statement[61] and the warrant must specifically describe the place to be searched, and the persons or things to be seized.

Amendment 5

Nobody may be tried for a crime that might be punishable by death, or for any other terrible crime, unless they are first indicted by a Grand Jury. The exceptions are cases involving the Army or Navy, and cases involving the Militia when they are actually serving during time of war or public danger.

Nobody may be tried twice for the same crime if the penalty could include loss of life or limb.[62] Nobody may be forced to testify against himself or herself in any criminal case. Nobody may be deprived of life, liberty, or property without proper operation of law. No private property may be taken for public use without fair compensation.

Amendment VI

In all criminal prosecutions, the accused shall enjoy the right to a speedy and public trial, by an impartial jury of the State and district wherein the crime shall have been committed, which district shall have been previously ascertained by law, and to be informed of the nature and cause of the accusation; to be confronted with the witnesses against him; to have compulsory process for obtaining witnesses in his favor, and to have the Assistance of Counsel for his defence.

Amendment VII

In Suits at common law, where the value in controversy shall exceed twenty dollars, the right of trial by jury shall be preserved, and no fact tried by a jury, shall be otherwise re-examined in any Court of the United States, than according to the rules of the common law.

Amendment VIII

Excessive bail shall not be required, nor excessive fines imposed, nor cruel and unusual punishments inflicted.

Amendment IX

The enumeration in the Constitution, of certain rights, shall not be construed to deny or disparage others retained by the people.

Amendment X

The powers not delegated to the United States by the Constitution, nor prohibited by it to the States, are reserved to the States respectively, or to the people.

Preamble and Text of Amendments 1-10 taken from:
http://www.archives.gov/exhibits/charters/bill_of_rights_transcript.html
Retrieved August 3, 2011

The Constitution Made Easy

Amendment 6

In all criminal cases, the accused person has the right to a speedy and public trial by an impartial jury from the State and district where the crime was committed. This district must have been previously determined by law. The accused person also has the right to be told exactly what the accusations are about, to confront the witnesses against him or her, to require witnesses in his or her favor to testify, and to have the assistance of a lawyer for his or her defense.

Amendment 7

In lawsuits under common law,[63] where the disputed amount is more than twenty dollars, the right of trial by jury will be preserved. No fact that has been tried by a jury, may be re-examined in any Court of the United States, except according to the rules of the common law.

Amendment 8

Excessive bail may not be required. Excessive fines may not be imposed. Cruel and unusual punishments may not be inflicted.

Amendment 9

The fact that certain rights of the people are listed in the Constitution does not mean that their other rights may be denied, or treated as less important.[64]

Amendment 10

The powers that are not delegated to the United States by the Constitution are retained by the separate States, or by the people. There are exceptions for certain powers that the Constitution prohibits to the States.[65]

Amendments 11-27

AMENDMENT XI *Passed by Congress March 4, 1794. Ratified February 7, 1795.* **Note:** *Article III, section 2, of the Constitution was modified by Amendment 11.*

The Judicial power of the United States shall not be construed to extend to any suit in law or equity, commenced or prosecuted against one of the United States by Citizens of another State, or by Citizens or Subjects of any Foreign State.

AMENDMENT XII *Passed by Congress December 9, 1803. Ratified June 15, 1804.* **Note:** *A portion of Article II, section 1 of the Constitution was superseded by the 12th Amendment.*

The Electors shall meet in their respective states and vote by ballot for President and Vice-President, one of whom, at least, shall not be an inhabitant of the same state with themselves;

they shall name in their ballots the person voted for as President, and in distinct ballots the person voted for as Vice-President, and they shall make distinct lists of all persons voted for as President, and of all persons voted for as Vice-President, and of the number of votes for each, which lists they shall sign and certify, and transmit sealed to the seat of the government of the United States, directed to the President of the Senate;

-- the President of the Senate shall, in the presence of the Senate and House of Representatives, open all the certificates and the votes shall then be counted; -- The person having the greatest number of votes for President, shall be the President, if such number be a majority of the whole number of Electors appointed;

and if no person have such majority, then from the persons having the highest numbers not exceeding three on the list of those voted for as President, the House of Representatives shall choose immediately, by ballot, the President. But in choosing the President, the votes shall be taken by states, the representation from each state having one vote; a quorum for this purpose shall consist of a member or members from two-thirds of the states, and a majority of all the states shall be necessary to a choice.

The Constitution Made Easy

Amendments 11-27

Amendment 11[66]

The judicial power of the United States will not include any kind of suit that is brought against one of the United States by citizens of any other State, or by citizens or subjects of any foreign State.

Amendment 12[67]

Section 1
The electors must meet in their respective States, and vote by ballot for President and Vice President. They may not vote for a President and a Vice President who are both from the same State as the electors.

Section 2
They must name in one set of ballots the person they voted for as President, and in a different set of ballots the person they voted for as Vice President. They must make separate lists of all the persons they voted for as President, and of all persons they voted for as Vice President, and the number of votes for each. They must sign these lists, and certify that they are correct, and send them sealed to the President of the Senate.

Section 3
The President of the Senate must open all the certificates in the presence of the Senate and House of Representatives, and the votes must then be counted. The person receiving the greatest number of votes for President will become the President, as long as he or she receives a majority of the total number of electors.

Section 4
If no person receives a majority, then the House of Representatives must immediately elect the President by ballot. They must choose him or her from the three persons with the highest numbers of votes. In choosing the President, the votes must be taken by States, and each State will have one vote. A quorum for this purpose will consist of at least one member from two-thirds of the States, and a majority of all the States will be necessary for the election to be final.

And if the House of Representatives shall not choose a President whenever the right of choice shall devolve upon them, before the fourth day of March next following, then the Vice-President shall act as President, as in case of the death or other constitutional disability of the President. – [Superseded by Section 3 of the 20th Amendment.]

[See Section 3 of the 20th Amendment]

The person having the greatest number of votes as Vice-President, shall be the Vice-President, if such number be a majority of the whole number of Electors appointed, and if no person have a majority, then from the two highest numbers on the list, the Senate shall choose the Vice-President; a quorum for the purpose shall consist of two-thirds of the whole number of Senators, and a majority of the whole number shall be necessary to a choice. But no person constitutionally ineligible to the office of President shall be eligible to that of Vice-President of the United States.

AMENDMENT XIII *Passed by Congress January 31, 1865. Ratified December 6, 1865.* **Note**: *A portion of Article IV, section 2, of the Constitution was superseded by the 13th amendment.*

Section 1.

Neither slavery nor involuntary servitude, except as a punishment for crime whereof the party shall have been duly convicted, shall exist within the United States, or any place subject to their jurisdiction.

Section 2.

Congress shall have power to enforce this article by appropriate legislation.

The Constitution Made Easy

Section 5[68]

If the President elect dies before the beginning of his or her term (Noon, January 20th), then the Vice President elect will become President. If a President has not been chosen before the beginning of his or her term, or if the President elect does not qualify, then the Vice President elect will act as President until a qualified President is chosen. [From A:20.3.1]

Section 6

In case neither a President elect, nor a Vice President elect qualifies, Congress may provide for this by law. Then this law will determine who will act as President, or the way in which the Acting President will be selected. This person will act as President until a qualified President or Vice President is chosen. [From A:20.3.2]

Section 7

The person receiving the greatest number of votes for Vice President will become the Vice President, as long as he or she receives a majority of the total number of electors. If no person receives a majority, then the Senate must choose the Vice President from the two persons with the highest numbers of votes. A quorum for this purpose will consist of two-thirds of the total number of Senators, and a majority of the total number will be necessary for the election to be final. If a person is not eligible, under the Constitution, to be President of the United States, that person will not be eligible to be Vice President either.

Amendment 13[69]

Section 1

Slavery and all other forms of involuntary service are forbidden within the United States, and all places under their authority, unless it is punishment for a crime for which the person has been properly convicted.

Section 2

Congress will have power to enforce this Amendment by appropriate laws.

AMENDMENT XIV *Passed by Congress June 13, 1866. Ratified July 9, 1868.* **Note:** *Article I, section 2, of the Constitution was modified by section 2 of the 14th amendment.*

Section 1.

All persons born or naturalized in the United States, and subject to the jurisdiction thereof, are citizens of the United States and of the State wherein they reside. No State shall make or enforce any law which shall abridge the privileges or immunities of citizens of the United States; nor shall any State deprive any person of life, liberty, or property, without due process of law; nor deny to any person within its jurisdiction the equal protection of the laws.

Section 2.

Representatives shall be apportioned among the several States according to their respective numbers, counting the whole number of persons in each State, excluding Indians not taxed. But when the right to vote at any election for the choice of electors for President and Vice-President of the United States, Representatives in Congress, the Executive and Judicial officers of a State, or the members of the Legislature thereof, is denied to any of the male inhabitants of such State, being twenty-one years of age, and citizens of the United States, or in any way abridged, except for participation in rebellion, or other crime, the basis of representation therein shall be reduced in the proportion which the number of such male citizens shall bear to the whole number of male citizens twenty-one years of age in such State. [Changed by the 19th and 26th Amendments.]

Section 3.

No person shall be a Senator or Representative in Congress, or elector of President and Vice-President, or hold any office, civil or military, under the United States, or under any State, who, having previously taken an oath, as a member of Congress, or as an officer of the United States, or as a member of any State legislature, or as an executive or judicial officer of any State, to support the Constitution of the United States, shall have engaged in insurrection or rebellion against the same, or given aid or comfort to the enemies thereof. But Congress may by a vote of two-thirds of each House, remove such disability.

<u>Amendment 14[70]</u>

Section 1

All people who are born or naturalized in the United States, and subject to their authority, are citizens of the United States and of the State they live in. No State may make or enforce any law which diminishes the privileges or freedoms of citizens of the United States. No State may take away any person's life, liberty, or property without proper operation of law. No State may deny any person under its authority the equal protection of the laws.

Section 2

The number of Representatives that each State has will be based upon the population of each State. For these purposes the population will count everybody except Indians who are not taxpayers. The right to vote may not be denied to any citizen in any State who is at least 18 years old.[71] This includes the right to vote for President and Vice President of the United States,[72] Representatives in Congress, as well as the Governor, judges and legislators of that State. If any State prevents or hinders any eligible citizen from voting, unless they participated in rebellion or other crime, the number of Representatives that State is entitled to will be reduced in proportion.

Section 3

Certain people are disqualified from being Senators or Representatives in Congress, or electors of President and Vice President, or holding any official position under the United States, or under any State.[73]

If they were ever a member of Congress, or a member of a State legislature, or an officer of the United States, or an official in any State; and took an oath to support the Constitution of the United States, and then they participated in revolution or rebellion against the Constitution, or if they gave assistance or support to its enemies, then they are disqualified. But Congress may make exceptions by a two-thirds vote of each House.

Section 4.

The validity of the public debt of the United States, authorized by law, including debts incurred for payment of pensions and bounties for services in suppressing insurrection or rebellion, shall not be questioned.

But neither the United States nor any State shall assume or pay any debt or obligation incurred in aid of insurrection or rebellion against the United States, or any claim for the loss or emancipation of any slave; but all such debts, obligations and claims shall be held illegal and void.

Section 5.

The Congress shall have the power to enforce, by appropriate legislation, the provisions of this article.

AMENDMENT XV *Passed by Congress February 26, 1869. Ratified February 3, 1870.*

Section 1.

The right of citizens of the United States to vote shall not be denied or abridged by the United States or by any State on account of race, color, or previous condition of servitude —

Section 2.

The Congress shall have the power to enforce this article by appropriate legislation.

AMENDMENT XVI *Passed by Congress July 2, 1909. Ratified February 3, 1913. **Note**: Article I, section 9, of the Constitution was modified by Amendment 16.*

The Congress shall have power to lay and collect taxes on incomes, from whatever source derived, without apportionment among the several States, and without regard to any census or enumeration.

AMENDMENT XVII *Passed by Congress May 13, 1912. Ratified April 8, 1913. **Note**: Article I, section 3, of the Constitution was modified by the 17th Amendment.*

The Senate of the United States shall be composed of two Senators from each State, elected by the people thereof, for six years; and each Senator shall have one vote. The electors in each State shall have the qualifications requisite for electors of the most numerous branch of the State legislatures.

The Constitution Made Easy

Section 4

The public debt of the United States is valid and may not be questioned if the debt was authorized by law. These debts include payment of pensions, and rewards for services used in suppressing revolution or rebellion.

But neither the United States, nor any State, may assume or pay any debt or obligation incurred as part of any revolution or rebellion against the United States. They may not pay any claim for the loss or freeing of any slave. All such debts, obligations and claims will be regarded as illegal and void.[74]

Section 5

Congress will have power to enforce the provisions of this Amendment by appropriate laws.

Amendment 15[75]

Section 1

The right of citizens of the United States to vote shall not be denied or diminished by the United States, or by any State, because of race, color, or previously being a slave.

Section 2

Congress will have power to enforce this Amendment by appropriate laws.

Amendment 16[76]

Congress will have power to assess and collect taxes on income from all sources. These taxes will not be based on the census, or divided proportionately between the States.

Amendment 17[77]

Section 1

The Senate of the United States will consist of two Senators from each State, elected by the people of that State, for six years; and each Senator will have one vote. Each State has a standard it uses to decide who is allowed to vote for its own State legislature. This same standard must be used to determine who is allowed to vote for members of the Senate.

When vacancies happen in the representation of any State in the Senate, the executive authority of such State shall issue writs of election to fill such vacancies: *Provided*, That the legislature of any State may empower the executive thereof to make temporary appointments until the people fill the vacancies by election as the legislature may direct.

This amendment shall not be so construed as to affect the election or term of any Senator chosen before it becomes valid as part of the Constitution.

AMENDMENT XVIII *Passed by Congress December 18, 1917. Ratified January 16, 1919. Repealed by Amendment 21.*

Section 1.

After one year from the ratification of this article the manufacture, sale, or transportation of intoxicating liquors within, the importation thereof into, or the exportation thereof from the United States and all territory subject to the jurisdiction thereof for beverage purposes is hereby prohibited.

Section 2.

The Congress and the several States shall have concurrent power to enforce this article by appropriate legislation.

Section 3.

This article shall be inoperative unless it shall have been ratified as an amendment to the Constitution by the legislatures of the several States, as provided in the Constitution, within seven years from the date of the submission hereof to the States by the Congress.

AMENDMENT XIX *Passed by Congress June 4, 1919. Ratified August 18, 1920.*

The right of citizens of the United States to vote shall not be denied or abridged by the United States or by any State on account of sex.

Congress shall have power to enforce this article by appropriate legislation.

The Constitution Made Easy

Section 2

When any Senator does not finish his or her term, the Governor from his or her State must set a Special Election to fill the remainder of that term. However, the legislature of that State may give the Governor power to make a temporary appointment that will only last until the position is filled by the Special Election.

Section 3

This Amendment may not be interpreted in a way that affects the election or term of any Senator who has already been elected when this Amendment becomes part of the Constitution.

Amendment 18

Section 1

One year after this Amendment receives final approval, it will be illegal to manufacture, sell, or transport alcoholic beverages within the United States, and United States territories. It will also be illegal to import or export alcoholic beverages into, or out of, the United States and United States territories. [Replaced by the 21st Amendment[78]]

Section 2

Congress and the separate States will all have power to make laws that enforce this Amendment.

Section 3

This Amendment will not go into effect unless it is approved by the legislatures of the various States, as described in the Constitution. The final approval process must also be completed within seven years from the date Congress sends it to the States.

Amendment 19[79]

Section 1

The right of citizens of the United States to vote shall not be denied or diminished by the United States, or by any State, because of gender.

Section 2

Congress will have power to enforce this Amendment by appropriate laws.

The Constitution of the United States

AMENDMENT XX *Passed by Congress March 2, 1932. Ratified January 23, 1933.* **Note:** *Article I, section 4, of the Constitution was modified by section 2 of this amendment. In addition, a portion of the 12th amendment was superseded by section 3.*

Section 1.

The terms of the President and the Vice President shall end at noon on the 20th day of January, and the terms of Senators and Representatives at noon on the 3d day of January, of the years in which such terms would have ended if this article had not been ratified; and the terms of their successors shall then begin.

Section 2.

The Congress shall assemble at least once in every year, and such meeting shall begin at noon on the 3d day of January, unless they shall by law appoint a different day.

Section 3.

If, at the time fixed for the beginning of the term of the President, the President elect shall have died, the Vice President elect shall become President. If a President shall not have been chosen before the time fixed for the beginning of his term, or if the President elect shall have failed to qualify, then the Vice President elect shall act as President until a President shall have qualified;

and the Congress may by law provide for the case wherein neither a President elect nor a Vice President shall have qualified, declaring who shall then act as President, or the manner in which one who is to act shall be selected, and such person shall act accordingly until a President or Vice President shall have qualified.

Section 4.

The Congress may by law provide for the case of the death of any of the persons from whom the House of Representatives may choose a President whenever the right of choice shall have devolved upon them, and for the case of the death of any of the persons from whom the Senate may choose a Vice President whenever the right of choice shall have devolved upon them.

The Constitution Made Easy

Amendment 20

Section 1[80]
The terms of the President and the Vice President will end at Noon on January 20th. The terms of Senators and Representatives will end at Noon on January 3rd. The terms of their successors will then begin. The years in which these various terms end, and others begin, is not changed by this Amendment.

Section 2[81]
Congress must meet at least once in every year, and the meeting will begin at Noon on January 3rd, unless the date is changed by Law.

Section 3[82]
20.3.1 If the President elect dies before the beginning of his or her term (Noon, January 20th), then the Vice President elect will become President. If a President has not been chosen before the beginning of his or her term, or if the President elect does not qualify, then the Vice President elect will act as President until a qualified President is chosen.

20.3.2 In case neither a President elect, nor a Vice President elect qualifies, Congress may provide for this by law. Then this law will determine who will act as President, or the way in which the Acting President will be selected. This person will act as President until a qualified President or Vice President is chosen.

Section 4
The right to choose the President may end up with the House of Representatives (see Amendment 12, Section 4). The right to choose the Vice President may end up with the Senate (see Amendment 12, Section 7). In either case, it is possible that one of the candidates could die before the House or Senate could vote. Congress may write a law to provide for this possibility.

Section 5.

Sections 1 and 2 shall take effect on the 15th day of October following the ratification of this article.

Section 6.

This article shall be inoperative unless it shall have been ratified as an amendment to the Constitution by the legislatures of three-fourths of the several States within seven years from the date of its submission.

AMENDMENT XXI *Passed by Congress February 20, 1933. Ratified December 5, 1933.*

Section 1.

The eighteenth article of amendment to the Constitution of the United States is hereby repealed.

Section 2.

The transportation or importation into any State, Territory, or Possession of the United States for delivery or use therein of intoxicating liquors, in violation of the laws thereof, is hereby prohibited.

Section 3.

This article shall be inoperative unless it shall have been ratified as an amendment to the Constitution by conventions in the several States, as provided in the Constitution, within seven years from the date of the submission hereof to the States by the Congress.

AMENDMENT XXII *Passed by Congress March 21, 1947. Ratified February 27, 1951.*

Section 1.

No person shall be elected to the office of the President more than twice, and no person who has held the office of President, or acted as President, for more than two years of a term to which some other person was elected President shall be elected to the office of President more than once. But this Article shall not apply to any person holding the office of President when this Article was proposed by Congress, and shall not prevent any person who may be holding the office of President, or acting as President, during the term within which this Article becomes operative from holding the office of President or acting as President during the remainder of such term.

The Constitution Made Easy

Section 5
Sections 1 and 2 shall take effect on the October 15th following the final approval of this Amendment.

Section 6
This Amendment will not go into effect unless it is approved by the legislatures of three-fourths of the States. The final approval process must also be completed within seven years from the date Congress sends it to the States.

Amendment 21

Section 1
This Amendment repeals (cancels out) the 18th Amendment of the Constitution.

Section 2
Alcoholic beverages may not be transported or imported into any State, Territory or Possession of the United States if it violates their laws, and if these beverages are going to be delivered or consumed there.

Section 3
This Amendment will not go into effect unless it is approved by the legislatures of the various States, as described in the Constitution. The final approval process must also be completed within seven years from the date Congress sends it to the States.

Amendment 22[83]

Section 1
No person may be elected to the office of President more than twice. If a person has already served as President or Acting President for more than two years of someone else's term, they may only be elected once. This Amendment will not apply to the person who is President or Acting President when this Amendment was proposed by Congress. If this Amendment is approved and becomes effective, it will not prevent the person who is President or Acting President at that time from finishing his or her term.

Section 2.

    This article shall be inoperative unless it shall have been ratified as an amendment to the Constitution by the legislatures of three-fourths of the several States within seven years from the date of its submission to the States by the Congress.

AMENDMENT XXIII *Passed by Congress June 16, 1960. Ratified March 29, 1961.*

Section 1.

    The District constituting the seat of Government of the United States shall appoint in such manner as Congress may direct:
A number of electors of President and Vice President equal to the whole number of Senators and Representatives in Congress to which the District would be entitled if it were a State, but in no event more than the least populous State; they shall be in addition to those appointed by the States, but they shall be considered, for the purposes of the election of President and Vice President, to be electors appointed by a State; and they shall meet in the District and perform such duties as provided by the twelfth article of amendment.

Section 2.

    The Congress shall have power to enforce this article by appropriate legislation.

AMENDMENT XXIV *Passed by Congress August 27, 1962. Ratified January 23, 1964.*

Section 1.

    The right of citizens of the United States to vote in any primary or other election for President or Vice President, for electors for President or Vice President, or for Senator or Representative in Congress, shall not be denied or abridged by the United States or any State by reason of failure to pay poll tax or other tax.

Section 2.

    The Congress shall have power to enforce this article by appropriate legislation.

The Constitution Made Easy

Section 2

This Amendment will not go into effect unless it is approved by the legislatures of three-fourths of the States. The final approval process must also be completed within seven years from the date Congress sends it to the States.

Amendment 23[84]

Section 1

Washington, D.C.[85] may appoint electors for President and Vice President in the way that Congress decides. The number of electors will be calculated as if this District was the State with the least population. These electors will be in addition to the ones appointed by the States, but they shall be treated the same as if they were appointed by a State for this purpose. They shall meet in the District and perform the same duties that are required of States by the 12th Amendment.

Section 2

Congress will have power to enforce this Amendment by appropriate laws.

Amendment 24[86]

Section 1

The right of citizens of the United States to vote shall not be denied or diminished by the United States, or by any State, for failure to pay a poll tax, or other tax. This right includes voting in primary elections, and other elections. It includes voting for President and Vice President,[87] and voting for Senators and Representatives in Congress.

Section 2

Congress will have power to enforce this Amendment by appropriate laws.

AMENDMENT XXV *Passed by Congress July 6, 1965. Ratified February 10, 1967. **Note**: Article II, section 1, of the Constitution was affected by the 25th amendment.*

Section 1.

In case of the removal of the President from office or of his death or resignation, the Vice President shall become President.

Section 2.

Whenever there is a vacancy in the office of the Vice President, the President shall nominate a Vice President who shall take office upon confirmation by a majority vote of both Houses of Congress.

Section 3.

Whenever the President transmits to the President pro tempore of the Senate and the Speaker of the House of Representatives his written declaration that he is unable to discharge the powers and duties of his office, and until he transmits to them a written declaration to the contrary, such powers and duties shall be discharged by the Vice President as Acting President.

Section 4.

Whenever the Vice President and a majority of either the principal officers of the executive departments or of such other body as Congress may by law provide, transmit to the President pro tempore of the Senate and the Speaker of the House of Representatives their written declaration that the President is unable to discharge the powers and duties of his office, the Vice President shall immediately assume the powers and duties of the office as Acting President.

Thereafter, when the President transmits to the President pro tempore of the Senate and the Speaker of the House of Representatives his written declaration that no inability exists, he shall resume the powers and duties of his office unless the Vice President and a majority of either the principal officers of the executive department or of such other body as Congress may by law provide, transmit within four days to the President pro tempore of the Senate and the Speaker of the House of Representatives their written declaration that the President is unable to discharge the powers and duties of his office.

Amendment 25[88]

Section 1

In case of the removal of the President from office, or of his or her death or resignation, the Vice President will become President.

Section 2

Whenever there is a vacancy in the office of the Vice President, the President must nominate a new Vice President. He will take office upon confirmation by a majority vote of both Houses of Congress.

Section 3

Whenever the President believes that he or she is unable to carry out the powers and duties of office, he or she may send written declaration to the temporary President of the Senate and to the Speaker of the House of Representatives. Until the President sends them a written declaration that he or she has become able again, these powers and duties must be discharged by the Vice President as Acting President.

Section 4

Whenever the Vice President and a majority of the Cabinet officers[89] agree that the President is unable to discharge the powers and duties of office, they may send their written declaration to the temporary President of the Senate and the Speaker of the House of Representatives. Then the Vice President must immediately assume the powers and duties as Acting President. (Congress may change this in the future from "the Cabinet" to some other group they designate by law.)

Section 5

After this, if the President believes that no inability exists, he or she must send written declaration to the temporary President of the Senate and to the Speaker of the House of Representatives. The President will resume the powers and duties of office unless the Vice President and a majority of the Cabinet officers oppose him or her. If they do, they must send their written declaration within four days to the temporary President of the Senate and to the Speaker of the House of Representatives reasserting that the President is unable to discharge the powers and duties of office.

Thereupon Congress shall decide the issue, assembling within forty-eight hours for that purpose if not in session. If the Congress, within twenty-one days after receipt of the latter written declaration, or, if Congress is not in session, within twenty-one days after Congress is required to assemble, determines by two-thirds vote of both Houses that the President is unable to discharge the powers and duties of his office, the Vice President shall continue to discharge the same as Acting President; otherwise, the President shall resume the powers and duties of his office.

AMENDMENT XXVI *Passed by Congress March 23, 1971. Ratified July 1, 1971. **Note**: Amendment 14, section 2, of the Constitution was modified by section 1 of the 26th amendment.*

Section 1.

The right of citizens of the United States, who are eighteen years of age or older, to vote shall not be denied or abridged by the United States or by any State on account of age.

Section 2.

The Congress shall have power to enforce this article by appropriate legislation.

AMENDMENT XXVII *Originally proposed Sept. 25, 1789. Ratified May 7, 1992.*

No law, varying the compensation for the services of the Senators and Representatives, shall take effect, until an election of representatives shall have intervened.

Text of Amendments 11-27 taken from:
http://www.archives.gov/exhibits/charters/constitution_amendments_11-27.html -- Retrieved August 3, 2011

The Constitution Made Easy

Section 6

At this point Congress must decide the issue. They must meet within 48 hours for this purpose if they are not already in session. Congress must make a determination within 21 days of receiving the most recent declaration (or 23 days if they were not in session). If Congress determines that the President is unable to discharge the powers and duties of office, then the Vice President will continue as Acting President. They must do this by two-thirds vote of both Houses. Otherwise, the President will resume the powers and duties of his or her office.

Amendment 26[90]

Section 1

The right of citizens of the United States to vote shall not be denied or diminished by the United States, or by any State, because of age, as long as they are eighteen years of age or older.

Section 2

Congress will have power to enforce this Amendment by appropriate laws.

Amendment 27[91]

No law that changes the pay of Senators and Representatives will take effect until after the next election of Representatives has taken place.

[1] This is known as the "Elector (voter) Qualification Clause." The original says, "for the most numerous Branch of the State Legislature." At the time it was possible that voting requirements could be different from one branch to the other. But as modified by various amendments, almost anyone over 18 years of age can now vote in virtually any election. See **C:1.2.3**, and the several amendments that affect it.

[2] *Legislature* means any "group of law-makers." In the Constitution, the term refers consistently to the law-makers of one or more of the States; *not* to Congress. Congress is first mentioned by saying it will have "all *legislative* Powers herein granted" (**C:1.1.1**). But after that introduction, they are consistently called *Congress*, or when just one House is in view, the *House of Representatives*, or the *Senate*. The Constitution frequently refers to Congress's power to *make law*, but never calls them a *legislature*.

[3] Every reference to *he, him, his*, etc. has been changed to gender-neutral or gender-inclusive terminology to show the effect of the 19th Amendment which gave women the right to vote in 1920.

[4] This Clause was superseded by Section 2 of the 14th Amendment, which has replaced nearly all of it here except for a few words concerning taxes, which the 14th Amendment did not address. The original text counted three-fifths of the slave population for both representation and taxation. This was known as the *three-fifths compromise*. In 1868, the 14th Amendment voided this formula, and added language about the right to vote. Several other amendments expanded this right.

[5] Under the original Constitution, all *direct taxes* had to be calculated in such a way that the amount each State paid was in proportion to its population (*apportioned*) (**C:1.9.4**). The 16th Amendment created an exception. See Amendment 16 and endnote.

[6] This sentence incorporates the effects of the 15th, 19th, 24th and 26th Amendments concerning race, gender, poll tax, and age.

[7] When voters cast their ballots for President and Vice President, they are actually choosing *electors* from their State (or from Washington, D.C.). These electors in turn vote for President and Vice President, as described in **C:2.1**.

[8] Congress determines the number of Representatives, provided that each State must have at least one, the number must be proportional to population, and there may not be more than one for every thirty thousand people. The number of Representatives rose steadily until 1911, when it was fixed at 435 where it remains today. Nothing in the Constitution prevents Congress from changing the number in the future.

[9] An *Impeachment* is a formal *charge* of wrongdoing that can only be brought by the House of Representatives, as indicated here. The actual trial to determine *guilt* takes place in the Senate (**C:1.3.7-8**).

[10] This paragraph is the text of **A:17.1**, which changed the method of electing Senators and added the qualifications of voters to be the same as for

---

Representatives. Prior to approval of the 17th Amendment in 1913, the Constitution required Senators to be chosen by their respective State legislatures.

[11] The original says, "for the most numerous Branch of the State Legislature." See **C:1.2.1** and endnote.

[12] This paragraph is the text of **A:17.2**, which modified the provisions for filling vacancies.

[13] The person who *presides* over something, whether it is a corporation, college, bank or government, is called the *President* of that entity. In the Constitution, *President* refers to the chief executive of the United States (see Article 2). The person who would take over his duties if he died, or became unable to continue in office, is called the *Vice President*. If the Vice President takes over, even temporarily, during that time he is called the *Acting President*. The Vice President is also the *President* of the Senate. He *presides* over it much of the time. When he is not there, the *President pro tempore* presides. The *President elect* and *Vice President elect* have been elected, but have not yet had their terms begin or taken their oaths of office. See 1.4.2 and Amendment 20 and the endnotes for more information on the time between elections and the beginnings of terms.

[14] The original phrase here is *pro tempore,* which means *temporary,* or *for the time.*

[15] According to Webster's 1828 Dictionary *Preside* means, "To be set over for the exercise of authority; to direct, control and govern, as the chief officer. A man may *preside* over a nation or province; or he may *preside* over a senate, or a meeting of citizens."

[16] An *Impeachment* is a formal *charge* of wrongdoing that can only be brought by the House of Representatives (**C:1.2.6**). The actual trial to determine *guilt* takes place in the Senate, as indicated here.

[17] The original says, "they shall be on Oath or Affirmation." Before conducting an impeachment trial, the Senators take an oath to act impartially as if they were judges or jurors. Generally, people who object to taking an oath in any court (often on religious grounds), may instead *affirm* that they will act impartially, or tell the truth, or whatever would have been expected if they had taken an oath.

[18] For example, an official could be *impeached* if he or she was accused of murder (or some other serious crime). If the House of Representatives *impeached* that official, and the Senate *convicted* him or her, the most they could do is remove the official from office, and ban him or her from future office. That would not let the official off the hook for the murder (or the other serious crime). He or she could, and most likely would, be arrested and tried by the proper authorities.

[19] The original adds an exception for the *place* of choosing Senators. At the time, Senators were chosen by State Legislatures, so it was important for States to retain autonomy over the *place* of those elections. The 17th Amendment changed the method of electing Senators to a popular election. There is no mention in the 17th Amendment of where the elections take place, or who has

final authority to decide this, but it is likely a moot point and so it was left out of this version.

[20] Some of this language is from the 20th Amendment which took effect in 1933. Until then, the date that the *terms* of Congress began and ended were simply set by law, not by the Constitution. For more information, see the 20th Amendment, Sections 1 and 2, and the endnotes.

[21] A *quorum* is the minimum number of persons that must be present for a group to conduct business. Often, as here, a majority is considered a *quorum*. But it can be a different number (**C:2.1.6** and **2.1.9**).

[22] *Adjourn* means to end a meeting, usually with a plan to reconvene at a later time, and/or in another place.

[23] The language about the change in pay is from the 27th Amendment (1992), and is included here.

[24] Courts have held that this protection generally extends only to civil arrests (which are virtually non-existent today), not criminal arrests. This portion of the Clause may be obsolete for all practical purposes.

[25] The original says "*general Welfare.*" The meaning here has to do with the mutual well-being of all the member States. This can be seen more clearly in the Articles of Confederation ("[the States] mutual and general welfare…", "for the defense and welfare of the United States, or any of them…"). Webster's 1828 Dictionary defines *Welfare* as, "Exemption from any unusual evil or calamity; the enjoyment of peace and prosperity, or the ordinary blessings of society and civil government; applied to states."

[26] These kinds of taxes were considered *indirect*. The Constitutional standard for *indirect taxes* was that they be *uniform* or consistent, the same everywhere. Contrast this with *direct taxes* which had to be *apportioned,* or in proportion to population (**C:1.9.4**).The 16th Amendment allowed Congress to assess an income tax, which is a *direct tax* that is *not based* upon population. Until this Amendment was ratified in 1913, all *direct taxes* were required to be *apportioned* (**C:1.9.4**). Income tax also affected **C:1.2.3**. The effect has been incorporated into those texts.

[27] Section 1 of the 14th Amendment expanded this Power by defining citizenship and adding federal protection for the rights of citizens.

[28] In the original, these letters of retaliation were called *Letters of Marque and Reprisal*. These letters were given by various governments to permit private citizens to do a number of things normally associated with the military. They could recover lost property, or use force to get even with the enemy for damages. They were sometimes authorized to capture enemies and enemy ships.

[29] *Captures* probably means *property* that was captured. But there is some evidence that the meaning might also include captured *people*, so it was not modernized, as any synonym might prejudice the meaning.

[30] There is much discussion about the meaning of the term *Militia* as it has evolved over the years. But at the time that the Constitution was drafted and ratified, nearly all able-bodied men in any State were considered to be part of

that State's Militia. They were expected to keep their own *arms*, and bring those arms with them to fight when needed, as they had just done during the Revolution. See also the 2nd Amendment and endnote.

[31] The original doesn't mention Washington, D.C. since that District had not yet been selected. Washington, D.C. (District of Columbia) has been "the Seat of the Government of the United States" since 1800. See also Amendment 23 and endnote.

[32] These are storage areas around a dock, especially for naval supplies.

[33] This Section includes limits on taxing, law-making and the United States Government in general. It also lists certain rights of citizens and State protections. There are substantial parallels to the Bill of Rights which expand on the same concepts.

[34] This was an oblique reference to the slave trade which was protected by this compromise for about twenty years. At the first Constitutionally-permitted opportunity, a federal law banning all future slave trade was passed by Congress and signed by President Thomas Jefferson. It became effective on January 1, 1808. Slavery itself was abolished by the 13th Amendment in 1865. The whole Clause may be obsolete, but it was retained here because it was changed by Law; not repealed or replaced by Amendment. Some State authority regarding immigration in general may remain.

[35] This right to be seen by a judge to determine whether a person is being properly held is called a *Writ of Habeas Corpus*.

[36] This kind of law was called a *Bill of Attainder*. It was an act of a legislature that found a person guilty, usually of treason. These bills have a very complex history, including putting people to death and then confiscating their property. Under the Constitution, Congress can set the penalty for treason (**C:3.3.2**), but guilt is determined by courts.

[37] These kinds of laws were called *ex post facto Laws*. That is the term used in the original. It means *after the fact*. So Congress may not decide that something *should have been* a crime, and make a law that goes backwards in time to punish the person(s) who did it.

[38] The Constitutional standard for *direct taxes* is that they be *apportioned*, meaning shared in proportion to each State's population. The income tax (allowed by the 16th Amendment in 1913) became the exception to that rule. See Amendment 16 and endnote.

[39] Many other countries at the time, including England, had *classes* of people. There were *nobles* of various ranks, such as duke, marquis, earl, viscount and baron. These people were regarded as having a higher rank in society than the rest, called *commoners*.

[40] Section 1 of the 14th Amendment contains additional prohibitions concerning what States may not do.

[41] *Letters of Marque and Reprisal*. See **C:1.8.11** and the endnote.

[42] *Bills of Attainder*. See **C:1.9.3** and the endnote.

[43] *Ex post facto Laws*. See **C:1.9.3** and the endnote.

[44] The original does not set any limit on the number of terms a President may serve. Since 1951, the 22nd Amendment has limited Presidents to being *elected* to two terms. It also allows for them to have previously served up to two years of someone else's term. See the 22nd Amendment for more detail.

[45] The original does not establish the beginning and ending of the President's term. This was simply set by law as March 4th until 1933 when the 20th Amendment changed it to January 20th, and made it part of the Constitution. Federal election dates are still set by law, and are presently the Tuesday after the first Monday in November in even-numbered years. A President is elected in every other Federal election, so if a year is divisible by four, there will be a Presidential election that year in November. The President will take office at Noon on January 20th of the following year.

[46] Originally, only the States appointed electors. In 1961, the 23rd Amendment gave Washington, D.C. the right to appoint some electors. For details, see **A:23**, and the endnote.

[47] The next seven Clauses are the full text of the 12th Amendment which superseded the original. The addition of these Clauses lengthens this section considerably over the original, and changes the numbering of the Clauses significantly. The method of electing the President was changed in 1804 by the 12th Amendment and again in 1933 by the 20th Amendment. Clauses **2.1.3** through **2.1.9** are the full text of the 12th Amendment, *as amended by* the 20th Amendment. So there are actually two paragraphs that appear in this Version three times: **A:20.3.1-2** became **A:12.5-6**, which became **C:2.1.7-8**.

[48] **C:2.1.12-13,** and **15-18** are the text of the 25th Amendment (1967). They supersede one simple paragraph in the original text about Presidential succession. The addition of these Clauses lengthens this Section considerably over the original, and changes the numbering of the Clauses significantly.

[49] This provision allows Congress to write laws that determine who will be President if *both* the President and Vice President become unable to serve for any reason. The law that currently determines this is called the Presidential Succession Act of 1947 (as amended). Under this law, the Speaker of the House of Representatives is next in line behind the Vice President. Then follows the President pro tempore of the Senate, the Secretary of State and the other members of the Cabinet.

[50] The actual language says "a majority of... the principal officers of the executive departments." These department heads are often referred to as the President's Cabinet or Cabinet officers.

[51] Two provisions in this Clause were nullified in 1795 by the 11th Amendment, and so they have been deleted here. Before the 11th Amendment, the Supreme Court also had authority over controversies between one State and citizens of a different State; and also between a State (or its citizens), and a foreign State (or its citizens).

[52] The original uses the phrase, *work corruption of blood.* Under *common law* (see Amendment 7 and the endnote), traitors would be executed and their

property would then be confiscated. This also had the effect of punishing the traitor's heirs, or bloodline.

[53] *General Laws* would be uniform from State to State, not specific to a certain case.

[54] The original had a Clause about returning slaves who escaped. This was nullified by the 13th Amendment in 1865, so that Clause is deleted here.

[55] In this paragraph various forms of the word "approve," replace various forms of the word "ratify," which appear in the original.

[56] The *Confederation* was the arrangement the States operated under before this Constitution was ratified (approved) in 1789. The *Articles of Confederation* was the agreement between the States that served much the same function as the Constitution. It was under this agreement that the *Confederacy* actually became known as *The United States of America*. It was drafted by the Second Continental Congress in 1777 and ratified (approved) by all 13 States in 1781, all while fighting the Revolutionary War. The framers of the Constitution met in Philadelphia in 1787 for the purpose of *amending* these *Articles*, and ended up drafting a brand new agreement. Here (**C:6.1**), the framers are reaffirming all debts and agreements made while they were operating under the *Articles of Confederation*.

[57] These first ten Amendments of the Constitution were proposed and ratified (approved) as a group. Some States refused to ratify the Constitution unless this *Bill of Rights* was promised. 12 Amendments were proposed by Congress, and these 10 were ratified effective December 15, 1791. One, concerning Congressional pay raises, was ratified over two hundred years later as the 27th Amendment.

[58] The original uses the term *arms*, which includes other military weapons and armor.

[59] For definition of *Militia*, see **C:1.8.15** and endnote.

[60] The original calls this reasonable belief *probable cause*. Just how *probable* the *cause* has to be for a warrant to be issued has been the subject of many court cases.

[61] The original says *oath* or *affirmation*. People who object to making a statement under oath (often on religious grounds), may instead *affirm* that they are telling the truth.

[62] This sentence only affected serious crimes in 1791. But in modern practice, this principle of "double jeopardy" has been extended by the courts to include all, or nearly all, crimes. This has had the effect of *increasing* the protection guaranteed by this Amendment.

[63] *Common law* is a big subject. But a short definition is that it is the unwritten law that has been universally accepted for a very, very long time.

[64] While some of the founders would not support the Constitution without a Bill of Rights, others opposed it on the grounds that listing a few of their rights, might cause their other rights to be "denied or disparaged." The Ninth Amendment was included to address this concern.

[65] The list of powers that the United States Government *does have* is contained in the Constitution. They are often referred to as *enumerated,* or numbered, powers. Most of them are listed in **C:1.8**. The list of powers the States *do not have* is also contained in the Constitution. Most of these are listed in **C:1.10**.

[66] The effect of the 11th Amendment on **C:3.2** has already been incorporated into the text of that Section.

[67] The 12th Amendment substantially affected **C:2.1**, superseding much of the original language. As a result, the entire Amendment has been duplicated and inserted into this Version as **C:2.1.3 to 2.1.9**.

[68] The next two Sections are actually **A:20.3.1-2** which superseded one sentence in the original.

[69] The effect of the 13th Amendment on **C:4.2.2** has already been incorporated into the text of that Clause. See also **C:1.9.1** and endnote.

[70] Section 1 of the 14th Amendment has the effect of adding new power for the United States to define citizenship and protect the freedoms of citizens (see **C:1.8.4**). It also limits what States may do as listed in **C:1.10**. Section 2 superseded **C:1.2.3**, and has already been duplicated and added there, virtually replacing that Clause except for a few words concerning taxes.

[71] This sentence also incorporates the effects of the 15th, 19th, 24th, and 26th Amendments concerning race, gender, poll tax, and age.

[72] When voters cast their ballots for President and Vice President, they are actually choosing *electors* from their State (or from Washington, D.C.). These electors in turn vote for President and Vice President, as described in **C:2.1**.

[73] This Section was designed to disqualify people who had held certain offices and then participated in the Civil War on the Side of the South.

[74] This Section affirms all debts incurred by the North in the Civil War; but nullifies all debts incurred by the South.

[75] The effect of the 15th Amendment on **A:14.2**, and on **C:1.2.3** has already been incorporated into those texts.

[76] The 16th Amendment had the effect of adding a new Power of Congress like those listed in **C:1.8**. It also affected **C:1.2.3** and **C:1.9.4**. The effect has been incorporated into those texts.

[77] The effects of the 17th Amendment on **C:1.3.1** and **C:1.3.3** have already been incorporated into those texts.

[78] It is often said that the 21st Amendment *repealed,* or cancelled out, the 18th Amendment, and Section 1 of the 21st Amendment says just that. But Section 2 then offers new language that has *Federal* implications for violating *State* laws concerning the transporting and importing of alcoholic beverages.

[79] The effect of the 19th Amendment on **A:14.2**, and on **C:1.2.3** has already been incorporated into those texts.

[80] Section 1 of the 20th Amendment establishes the *terms* for President, Vice President, Senators and Representatives. The effect on the President's term was incorporated into **C:2.1.1**. (The President's term was restated for clarity in Section 3 of this Version.)

---

[81] Section 2 of the 20th Amendment establishes the first *meeting* date of Congress in each year. Sections 1 and 2 affected **C:1.4.2** and the effects have been incorporated there. Until the 20th Amendment took effect in 1933, the date that the *terms* of Congress and the President began and ended were simply set by law, not by the Constitution. From the beginning, Congress set that date as March 4. The Constitution set the first *meeting* date as "the first Monday in December," so nine months would elapse between the start of the term and the first meeting. A few more months would elapse between Federal *elections* and the start of the *term*. So a full year could elapse between the *elections* and the first *meeting*. Because of the 20th Amendment, there is a much shorter time between Congressional elections and the date their terms begin. Their first meeting is now set for the same day as the start of their term. (The first meeting date, but not the date the term begins, may still be changed by law). Similarly, the President's term now begins on January 20th.

[82] Section 3 of the 20th Amendment superseded Section 5 of the 12th Amendment. The 12th Amendment had already superseded several Clauses in Article 2, Section 1. The 12th Amendment, as amended by the 20th Amendment, is seen again in this Version as **C:2.1.3-9**. See **C:2.1.3-9**, and Amendment 12, and the endnotes.

[83] The effect of this Amendment on **C:2.1.1** has already been incorporated into the text of that Clause.

[84] The effect of this Amendment on **C:2.1.2** has already been incorporated into the text of that Clause.

[85] The original calls Washington, D.C. "the District constituting the seat of Government of the United States." Washington, D.C. (District of Columbia) has been the seat of Government of the United States since 1800.

[86] The effect of this Amendment on **A:14.2**, and on **C:1.2.3** has already been incorporated into those texts.

[87] When voters cast their ballots for President and Vice President, they are actually choosing *electors* from their State (or from Washington, D.C.). These electors in turn vote for President and Vice President, as described in **C:2.1**.

[88] This Amendment substantially affected **C:2.1**, superseding some of the original language. As a result, the entire Amendment has been duplicated and inserted into this version as **C:2.1.12-13, 15-18**.

[89] The actual language says "a majority of... the principal officers of the executive departments." These department heads are often referred to as the President's Cabinet or Cabinet officers.

[90] The effects of this Amendment on **A:14.2** and **C:1.2.3** have already been incorporated into those texts.

[91] This Amendment affected **C:1.6.1**, and the effects have been incorporated. It was proposed as one of the original Bill of Rights, but it was not approved until over two hundred years later, which was possible because there was no deadline set for ratification. Some more recent Amendments have set seven-year deadlines for ratification.

Recommended Resources

Many of these resources are available online and in print. One online resource may be suggested, but there are usually others that can be easily found using any standard search engine.

Blackstone, William, Sir. *Commentaries on the Laws of England*. Oxford: Clarendon Press, 1765-1769. (Note: This version is available online at the Avalon Project of Yale Law School. http://avalon.law.yale.edu/subject_menus/blackstone.asp)
    For the very serious student who wishes to understand the fundamentals of English law that provided much of the legal framework and background that the framers of the Constitution would have been familiar with.

Farrand, Max, ed. *The Records of the Federal Convention of 1787*. New Haven: Yale University Press, 1911. 3 vols. (Note: This version is available at the Online Library of Liberty. http://oll.libertyfund.org/index.php?option=com_staticxt&staticfile=show.php?title=1785&Itemid=27)
    Once again, this is a resource for the serious student because of its size; but anyone can enjoy perusing excerpts. Includes the notes of James Madison which have also been published separately. A later "Supplement" to these records is also available from Yale University Press.

Hamilton, Alexander et al. *The Federalist*. Benjamin Fletcher Wright, ed. New York: Barnes and Noble, 2004.
(Note: Another version is available at the Online Library of Liberty. http://oll.libertyfund.org/index.php?option=com_staticxt&staticfile=show.php%3Ftitle=788&Itemid=27)
    This is a standard volume for students of the Constitution. One or more versions are available at most bookstores. Contains the arguments of Alexander Hamilton, James Madison and John Jay as they wrote (under the collective pseudonym of *Publius*) in favor of ratifying the new Constitution.

The Constitution Made Easy -Endnotes

Hirsch, E.D. *Validity in Interpretation*. New Haven: Yale University Press, 1967.
> A standard work on the principles of literary interpretation.

Ketcham, Ralph, ed. *The Anti-Federalist Papers and the Constitutional Convention Debates*. New York: New American Library - Signet Classics, 2003. (Note: Similar information is available online at http://www.constitution.org/afp/afp.htm)
> This collection is reader friendly and includes many of the best portions of the larger compilations by Farrand and Storing.

Meese III, Edwin, ed. *The Heritage Guide to the Constitution*. Washington, DC: Regnery Publishing Company, 2005.
> This is an almost line-by-line commentary on the Constitution from a number of contributors who generally observe the originalist perspective. Relevant court cases are also frequently cited and discussed.

Storing, Herbert J. *The Complete Anti-Federalist*. Chicago: University of Chicago Press, 1981.
> Several American patriots gave speeches and wrote articles opposing the approval of the new Constitution, believing that the *Articles of Confederation* were sufficient for an alliance of independent States. These writers generally wrote under pseudonyms, but included Patrick Henry and other well-known figures of the Revolution. Storing also published an excerpted version in 1985 called simply, *The Anti-Federalist*.

Story, Joseph. *Commentaries on the Constitution of the United States*. Boston: Hilliard, Gray and Company, 1833.
(Note: This version is available online at The Constitution Society. www.constitution.org/js/js_000.htm)

Webster, Noah. *American Dictionary of the English Language 1828*. Reprinted Chesapeake Virginia: FACE Publishing, 1968.
(Note: Online word searches available at: http://1828.mshaffer.com/)
> This dictionary was published less than 40 years after the drafting of the Constitution and captures the meaning of the words as they were used at the time more closely than later dictionaries.

Thanks:

The author wishes to thank his family for their help and sacrifice, and for putting up with the long hours involved in this project. To Cat: You have always believed in me, and I owe it all to you. To Denae, Mary, Levi and AmyJoy: Daddy loves you and owes you a special day.

Debts of gratitude are owed to Kirk DouPonce at DogEared Design for an incredible job on the book cover, and Dennis Cheaqui at GD Printing and Graphics for many extra hours typesetting and printing to almost impossible standards.

Special thanks also to the many proof-readers involved in this project, including Stephen Amy, Tony Holler, David Pagard, Jeffery Price, Mick Tillman and especially the 7th graders at CSCS Woodland Park, including the author's daughter, Mary Holler, and her classmate Heidi Bacorn.

About the Author:

Mike Holler is an alumnus of both the Master's College and Biola University, where he studied literary interpretation and translation.

He lives with his wife Cathy and four of their seven children in the mountains of Colorado. Mike is a freelance writer and speaker, as well as a frequent guest and guest host on radio. He travels regularly with the Tea Party Express and is available to speak on the subject of the United States Constitution virtually anywhere in the United States.

Inquiries:

For speaking engagements or other inquiries please contact the author directly via email: MikeHoller@aol.com.

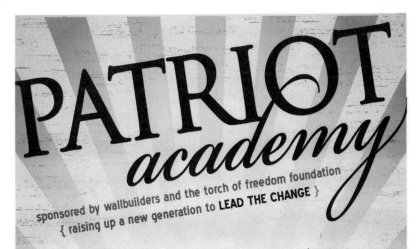

PATRIOT *academy*

sponsored by wallbuilders and the torch of freedom foundation
{ raising up a new generation to **LEAD THE CHANGE** }

CHALLENGE YOUR IDEA OF GOVERNMENT

At Patriot Academy, you don't just learn about government, you live it. This summer, you and your fellow students, ages 16-25, will take over the Texas state government at the Capitol Building in Austin, Texas. You will work together to form a fully functioning mock government, drafting legislation, running committee meetings, debating bills, electing leaders and passing laws.

CONFRONT THE ISSUES OF TODAY

In a fast-paced, interactive format, elected officials and experts will explain today's most relevant issues. Through media relations training, public speaking workshops and spirited debate, you will learn to articulate what you believe and why. Patriot Academy will equip you to effect change for the issues that matter most to you, whether as a concerned citizen or political candidate.

CHAMPION THE CAUSE OF FREEDOM

If you want to be a part of a new generation of young leaders poised to change the future of American politics, join us at Patriot Academy. You won't want to miss it!

FOR MORE INFORMATION OR TO APPLY, VISIT US AT
WWW.PATRIOTACADEMY.COM

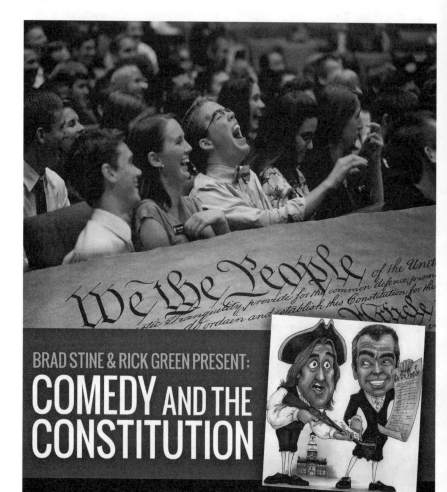

BRAD STINE & RICK GREEN PRESENT:
COMEDY AND THE CONSTITUTION

Brad Stine

Rick Green

Laugh & Learn with Brad Stine ("God's Comic") and Rick Green (WallBuilders speaker & radio host, founder of Patriot Academy) as they use hilarious history to bring America's founding documents to life.

Freedom is not a boring subject... especially when comedian Brad Stine is in the mix! This one of a kind approach to history will leave a lasting impression on your congregation and move them to action as they live out their freedom with a Biblical Worldview.

Have you ever wondered how legends came into being? Have you ever desired to learn from the legends of history? Have you ever desired to become a legend? 12 authors bring you stories of courage, mentorship & virtue through *Legends of Liberty*!

Legends of Liberty tells the story of 15 legends throughout history and teaches the reader how to emulate their actions in modern society. Each chapter is written by a different author, each a modern day legend in their own right.

Legends of Liberty is edited, compiled, and formulated by Rick Green. Contributing authors include David Barton, Gary Newell, Cliff Graham, Krish Dhanam, Timothy Barton, Brad Stine, Paul Tsika, Alexandra Murphy, and many others!

Legends and stories told include John Locke, King David, Nathan Hale, Squanto, Zig Zigler, Sybil Ludington, Brian Birdwell, Jimmy Robertson, Divey Langston, Moe Berg, and many others!

Get your Patriot Boot Camp in a Box at PatriotAcademy.com

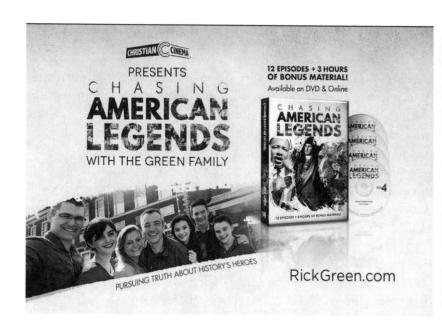

ABOUT THE AUTHOR...

Rick is known as America's Constitution Coach. He is a former Texas State Representative, attorney, author, and nationally recognized speaker on the Constitution and America's founding principles. He currently co-hosts the daily radio talk show *WallBuilders Live! w/David Barton*. Rick and his wife, Kara, and their children travel the Nation together teaching on the Constitution and inspiring citizens to do their part in protecting our cherished freedoms. They bring history to life with their fun and entertaining adventures in their *Chasing American Legends* reality television series.

Connect with the Green family at PatriotAcademy.com for regular updates, articles, and liberty inspiring information!

Get the FULL Constitution Alive
Course Package & Share with Others!

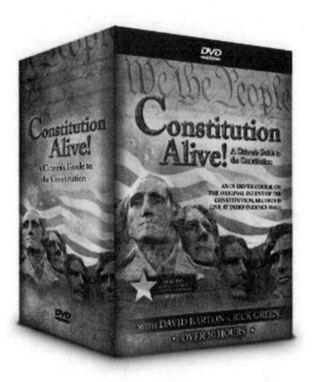

Recorded live in the very cradle of liberty, Independence Hall in Philadelphia, as well as all the additional sessions with David Barton in the amazing WallBuilders Library. Includes Q&A from attendees and teaching from Rick's four children. Available on DVD or digital access with digital workbook. Order today at **PatriotAcademy.com**.

YOU can be the catalyst to restore Biblical & Constitutional principles in your community. Sign up today to become a Constitution Coach. Includes training on hosting classes online or in person, and a broadcast license to share these powerful materials with as many people as you can!

Visit **BiblicalCitizens.com** to learn more!